INDIA AHEAD

INDIA AHEAD
2025 and Beyond

BIMAL JALAN

RUPA

First published by
Rupa Publications India Pvt. Ltd 2018
7/16, Ansari Road, Daryaganj
New Delhi 110002

Sales Centres:

Allahabad Bengaluru Chennai
Hyderabad Jaipur Kathmandu
Kolkata Mumbai

Copyright © Bimal Jalan 2018

The views and opinions expressed in this book are the author's own and the facts are as reported by him which have been verified to the extent possible, and the publishers are not in any way liable for the same.

All rights reserved.
No part of this publication may be reproduced, transmitted, or stored in a retrieval system, in any form or by any means, electronic, mechanical, photocopying, recording or otherwise, without the prior permission of the publisher.

ISBN: 978-93-5304-591-3

First impression 2018

10 9 8 7 6 5 4 3 2 1

The moral right of the author has been asserted.

Printed by Parksons Graphics Pvt.Ltd., Mumbai.

This book is sold subject to the condition that it shall not, by way of trade or otherwise, be lent, resold, hired out, or otherwise circulated, without the publisher's prior consent, in any form of binding or cover other than that in which it is published.

*To
Maahira and Ayushman,
Ananmay and Tanay,
the future is yours to make...*

Contents

Introduction / ix

1. A Definitive Agenda for Political Reforms / 1
2. Preserving Unity in Diversity in the Parliament / 30
3. Criminals in Politics / 47
4. Corruption Multiplier / 57
5. Enhancing the Quality of Life / 77
6. A New Paradigm for the Financial Sector / 91
7. The Role of Government and Administrative Reforms / 112
8. The Twenty-first Century Is India's Century / 127
9. Epilogue: The India of Our Dreams / 136

Acknowledgements / 153

Index / 155

Introduction

There is no doubt that opportunities for India to accelerate its growth rate further (say, to 8 per cent or more) and eliminate poverty by improving the Public Distribution System (PDS) are much better now than was the case at any time in the past. There are very few developing countries that are as well placed as India to take advantage of the fundamental changes that have occurred in production technologies, international trade, capital movement and employment of skilled manpower. At the same time, all observers of the Indian economy, including governments in power, also generally agree that in order to realize its full potential in the new global environment, it is necessary for India to make decisive moves towards deeper reforms and reduce the pervasive and procedural political and administrative bottlenecks.

In recent years, the global environment has also changed in India's favour. In the latest report of the World Bank in 2018, on ease of doing business, India's rank jumped thirty places to 100, from 130 a year ago. India has also been adjudged the fifth best-performing nation globally in reforming the business environment. As never before, India's destiny is now truly in its people's hands. With our determination to realize the country's vast potential, India's economy can become one of the strongest in the world in the not-too-distant future. Widespread poverty, illiteracy and disease would then largely disappear and democracy would have given the people their just rewards.

This book deals with certain priorities for India in the long run, i.e. up to 2025. It takes a longer-term perspective on the country's prospects and the many challenges that need to be tackled in order to realize its full potential for high growth combined with the alleviation of poverty. Some of these long-term priorities could also be launched by the present government, which, for the first time after 1989, has the advantage of having a majority of its own in the Parliament. However, all these suggestions are also likely to be relevant for any party (or coalition of parties) that comes to power in 2019.

It must be clarified that most of the challenges that have been highlighted in the different chapters of this book may take some time to be resolved. However, their resolution is not dependent on which party, or coalition of parties, is in power over time and its ideological or electoral agenda. The primary focus of the book is on promoting India's national interest in the long run, irrespective of a party's specific political agenda—either on the right or the left (or a mix of both).

India's fundamentals are, no doubt, stronger now than ever before, but it also faces several old and new challenges in the areas of politics, economics and governance. These challenges can only be met if we are able to generate sufficient political will to pursue the right policies and shake off the dead weight of the past.

The first three chapters deal with different aspects of the political scenario such as political corruption or political opportunism. Some of these are carry-overs from the past and not necessarily related either to earlier coalition governments or

Introduction

the present government. There is considerable public and media discussion of each aspect, particularly when some high-profile event occurs, such as the accumulation of illicit wealth by former chief ministers and Union ministers. However, there isn't sufficient appreciation of the fact that, taken as a whole, there have been some basic and fundamental changes in the functioning of India's democracy in recent years, which can be ignored only at our peril. These changes are important enough to call for political reforms in the conduct of business in the Parliament and other organs of the State.

The first chapter, 'Definitive Agenda for Political Reforms', outlines certain priorities to make the present system more accountable and strengthen the democratic process by improving the functioning of different agencies of the State, particularly the Parliament and the government, to ensure the speedy implementation of public policies. Some of the issues that need to be confronted as early as possible, include:

- Review of the present division of administrative powers between the Union and the states. This will ensure better implementation of development programmes and allocation of Centre's budgetary resources to states, for financing specific subsidies and other projects.
- Reform of the present system of election to the Rajya Sabha. This will ensure that those who are elected by different states as its members, actually represent the views of their states during discussions for the approval of legislations and other policy measures in the Upper House.
- Introduction of a practical and equitable scheme for State funding of elections and distribution of electoral funds

among large and small political parties.
- Parliamentary proceedings to be made more orderly and the Speaker/Chairman of the two Houses need to be empowered, so as to mandatorily suspend or expel members who frequently disrupt proceedings or functioning.
- Redefine the political role of the government in implementation of announced economic policies in order to ensure a suitable and competitive environment with a strong external sector and a transparent domestic financial system.
- In order to simplify the present complex administrative procedures, a distinction should be made between the ownership of public services by the government and delivery of such services by Non-governmental Organizations (NGOs) and local enterprises. The government can, of course, retain the responsibility for regulating and monitoring the performance of public authorities.
- Judicial delays in India are now legendary. A delay of ten to fifteen years in settling even the most blatant and clear-cut violation of law is quite common. It is now essential to reform the legal system to reduce the scope of appeals, adjournments and frequent hearings at different levels of the judiciary.
- In order to improve the functioning of civil services, there should be a separation of powers within the executive: between ministers and civil servants with regards to postings, transfers, promotions and other similar administrative matters. The greater empowerment of the civil services must, of course, go hand in hand with the greater accountability of civil servants for their performance and conduct.

Introduction

Sixteen years ago, in 2002, the National Commission to review the working of the Constitution (NCRWC) had highlighted the increasing concern in the media and the people about the 'decline of the Parliament's standards of debate, erosion of the moral authority and prestige of the supreme tribute of the people'.[1] Since then, there is very little doubt that the functioning of the Parliament, if anything, has worsened and disputes between the leading party and coalition parties have increased substantially.

Thus, Chapter 2, 'Preserving Unity in Diversity in the Parliament', discusses the working of the Parliament. It examines, in detail, some of the issues relating to parliamentary procedures and the role of small parties, which require to be tackled when, for the first time after 1989, India has a government in power which has a majority of its own in the Lok Sabha.

The chapter also highlights the developments that took place in the Parliament over five days—between 18 and 22 March—during the Budget session of 2006. I had the opportunity to watch these extremely distressing events at close quarters as a nominated member of the Rajya Sabha at that time. During this period, a number of unprecedented decisions were announced by the government regarding the business agenda in the two Houses which were passively accepted by both of them. Not only was the finance bill for the fiscal year 2007–08 approved by a voice vote in the midst of noise and disruption, but nearly a hundred other papers, which were laid on the table of the House, were also approved within just four minutes.

The above developments are symptomatic of the diminishing role of the Parliament in the conduct of the nation's affairs, and the

---

[1] Summary Of Recommendations. (2002, April 01). Retrieved from https://www.outlookindia.com/website/story/summary-of-recommendations /215076

power of the government to do what it wishes to do, irrespective of actual outcomes on the ground. In the long term, for the better functioning of the Parliament, it is important to make necessary constitutional amendments to confer adequate powers to the Chairs of the two Houses to control the unruly behaviour of the opposition parties or members.

It will be desirable to make the anti-defection law applicable to all small parties, and not just individual members. At present, this law applies to any member of a political party who wishes to join another party. The unintended effect of this has been the fragmentation of political parties into multitudes of separate small parties with leaders who may have influence in just a few constituencies.

Next, Chapter 3, titled 'Criminals in Politics', discusses what can be done to reduce the incentives for convicted criminals on bail, such as contesting elections. An important reform which can be introduced, perhaps after the general elections of 2019, is to reverse this incentive.

An amendment in election laws must be introduced so that the 'presumed' innocence of elected persons is given precedence. Such cases may be heard in courts, say within six months, before they take their seats in the assembly or Parliament. A fast settlement of these cases would provide relief to persons who are actually innocent and not only 'presumed' to be so. At the same time, it will discourage persons who are actually guilty from contesting elections and thereby delay hearings of their cases!

Several positive actions have been taken by the present and earlier governments to reduce the number of convicted criminals who are nominated by different political parties to contest elections and thereby reduce the level of corruption in the administrative and political system.

Introduction

It is not generally appreciated that the adverse effect of high corruption on the country's income, fiscal balance and investment is a 'multiple' of the amount of actual illicit monetary benefits to the corrupt. Empirical research shows that for every rupee of monetary gain to the corrupt, the aggregate loss to society could be as high as three or four rupees. Chapter 4, 'Corruption Multiplier', examines the consequences of high corruption on India's economy, and what can be done to substantially improve its rank in the Global Corruption Barometer over the next few years.

In light of the damaging effects of the corruption multiplier—not only in terms of income distribution, but also on factor productivity, delays in completion of public projects, inflation and effectiveness of fiscal policies—this chapter outlines certain important measures to reduce the supply and demand of corruption. The priority, thus, in the current situation is to ensure transparency in the decision-making process and full disclosure of decisions actually taken by different ministries to implement macroeconomic policies announced by the government, particularly on matters that have financial implications.

There is no doubt that high levels of corruption have also adversely affected the delivery of public services to the poor across the country and has reduced India's rank in the Human Development Index (HDI), which is computed by the United Nations Development Programme (UNDP). Chapter 5, titled 'Enhancing the Quality of Life', deals with India's record in the social sectors and highlights some of the important issues which need to be tackled by India in the future, in respect of three priority areas of social importance—nutrition, life expectancy and literacy—which are used to measure the rank of different countries on the HDI.

The chapter outlines certain principles which need to be

observed by India in organizing faster delivery of social services to the poor. In respect of food security, for example, the 'distribution' of food is as important as its production. The challenge of the future is to substantially widen the reach of the PDS among the poor and make it more cost-effective and equitable. Similarly, in order to achieve the goals of universal literacy, priority should be given to significantly increasing financial support by the Centre for elementary education rather than higher education in colleges and universities across the country.

Certain organizational reforms should also be introduced to improve the delivery system for healthcare. One such reform that deserves to be implemented is to decentralize delivery of health services to states and districts. Decentralization is potentially the most important force for improving efficiency and responding to local healthcare conditions and demands.

For the effective decentralization of public services, it is, thus, desirable to provide adequate financial authority to local bodies to implement social programmes assigned to them. Decentralization of financial powers, with appropriate audit requirements and performance monitoring, can contribute substantially to improving the quality of primary education and healthcare in rural areas and strengthening the accountability of local institutions. It will also facilitate greater participation by the community through NGOs, in the delivery of social services to the poor.

The critical role of the financial system in determining the stability and sustainability of the real economy became evident during the Asian financial crisis of 1997–99. Against the backdrop of the invaluable lessons from the crisis, Chapter 6, 'New Paradigm for the Financial Sector', deals with certain issues relating to the substantial growth in the depth and widening of the financial sector in India in recent years, and the policy framework for the future.

Introduction

In 2017–18, despite several highly positive measures taken by the government, economic growth witnessed some downturn. The growth rate in the previous year was 6.7 per cent, rather than the 7–8 per cent which was the case in the first three years of the present government (2014–15, 2015–16, 2016–17). India's investment to Gross Domestic Product (GDP) ratio has also slipped significantly from over 35 per cent in the last eight years to below 30 per cent.

This can be partly explained by risk aversion among banks in view of the high levels of Non-performing Assets (NPAs). There has also been a significant decline in private corporate revenues and investment. As yet, it is not clear whether the decline in growth and investment is cyclical or structural. The immediate priority for the government is to take strong measures to improve the growth and investment climate.

Some of the priority areas where long-term reforms and policy initiatives are required to achieve India's full potential as an emerging global power by 2025 are outlined in Chapter 7—'The Role of Government and Administrative Reforms'. Recasting the role of the government in the economy and introducing some important administrative reforms in the next few years would provide substantial opportunity for India to achieve, in the first quarter of the twenty-first century, what could not be achieved in the previous fifty or hundred years.

In recent years, the patterns of trade and investment have also moved in India's favour. India's competitive advantage no longer lies only in the production of low-value, low-technology, labour-intensive goods, but also in relatively high-value, skill-intensive and high-technology products and services.

Chapter 8 of the book, 'The Twenty-first Century Is India's Century', and the epilogue, 'The India of Our Dreams', identify some important issues that need to be tackled for us to realize India's full potential in the global economy.

The overarching conclusion of this book, which I hope will be of particular interest to readers, is simply that India's opportunities are huge, and so are the challenges which need to be resolved to realize its full potential. My fervent hope, as outlined in this book, is that India's participative and democratic system will ensure the collective cooperation needed to make the economy stronger, and its politics more people-oriented. In future, by 2025, if there is sufficient will and cooperation among different branches of the government, i.e. legislature, judiciary and executive, it should be potentially less difficult to find solutions to the problems that India faces.

1
A Definitive Agenda for Political Reforms

I have often called for minimum government, maximum governance. This is not a slogan. This is an important principle to transform India... First, we need to focus [the] government upon the things that are required of the State. Second, we need to achieve competence in government so that the State delivers on the things it sets out to do...[1]

—Prime Minister Narendra Modi,
16 January 2015

The Modi-led government, owing to its majority, has the ability to bring some important reforms not only in economic policies but also in respect of the working of the political and administrative system, which can deliver public services to all,

---

[1] ET Global Business Summit 2015. (2015, January 16). Retrieved from https://economictimes.indiatimes.com/slideshows/corporate-industry/etglobal-business-summit-2015/slideshow/45916013.cms

with least diversion, delay or multi-tier corruption in allocation.

It hardly needs to be emphasized that a fundamental 'systemic' change, which dominates the working of India's politics today—unlike the first four decades after Independence—is the fragmentation of political parties. As a result, India has had as many as nine governments in the past twenty-five years—with an average life of about two and a half years. Of these, only two coalitions survived their five-year terms. Excluding these two full-term coalition governments, the average term of seven governments—with enormous powers to allocate resources, control public enterprises and decide interstate allocation of investments—was less than two years. The crucial point, in view of past experience, is that at the time of the formation of a coalition government, the general expectation of small and regional parties is that the enormous powers that their nominees, as ministers, enjoy, may not last very long—or that it may change if a more powerful leader of one or two large parties in the coalition so decides.

The proposed agenda for political reforms outlined in this chapter, is necessarily selective and not comprehensive. I have no illusion that the proposed changes to make the present system more accountable and strengthen the democratic process would be easy to accept or implement, because of the inherent conflicts of interest among different sections of the political spectrum. However, I believe that this is a minimum—and practical—agenda that deserves consideration and debate in legislative bodies, media and other institutions of the civil society. The next Lok Sabha elections will be held in 2019 and once these suggestions have been debated and approved, the implementation of reforms can take place over time.

A Federation of States

Articles 245 to 255 of the Constitution of India deal with the distribution of powers between the Union and the states. The Centre has exclusive powers to make laws in respect of matters enumerated in the Union List (such as defence, foreign relations and financial matters concerning the whole of India). The states, on the other hand, have exclusive powers to make laws in respect of matters enumerated in the State List. These generally include matters where uniformity across the different states in respect of legal and administrative matters is not considered necessary (such as internal law and order, agriculture, trade and commerce, within a state).

There is also the Concurrent List under which both the Union and the states can make laws. These include matters where the Centre can make laws applicable to all of India, but where individual states are also entitled to pass laws of specific interest to them. The residual powers, i.e. powers to make laws on any subject that is not listed in any of the above lists, rest with the Union (unlike certain other federations, such as the United States [US], where the residual powers are with the states). The Centre also has the powers to make laws that are applicable to two or more states, if the concerned states so request, on a matter listed in the State List.

The above scheme for the distribution of powers between the Union and the states has stood the test of time and is a tribute to the foresight of the framers of India's Constitution. In a country with such great diversity in languages, religions, castes and levels of development, this scheme also proved to be a major unifying force among different states. All states are represented in the two Houses of the Parliament and work together on the treasury benches or in the Opposition. Regional issues and matters of interest to particular states are open to discussion in the Parliament and are generally resolved through a consensus.

There are, of course, long-standing interstate disputes (particularly on water or sources of energy), which flare up from time to time. However, even these have not threatened the unity of India because of the Union's conciliatory role and the representation of most states in the Union Cabinet. An outstanding initiative taken last year by the government was the introduction of the Goods and Services Tax (GST) with mutual agreement between the Centre and the states.

In the context of recent political developments at the Centre and the emergence of multiparty coalitions of different types and durations as a regular feature of governments, it is perhaps now necessary to also review the present division of powers between the Union and the states. In view of external terrorist linkages and other factors, there is an urgent need to consider transfer of powers for the maintenance of internal security to the Centre from the states.

In the economic area, it is desirable to consider a reverse transfer, i.e. the powers and responsibility for financing development programmes should be transferred from the Centre to the states. At present, the states formulate their plans, but the responsibility for the approval and provision of sufficient resources for implementing them rests with the Centre.

In the context of coalition politics, an investment plan for a particular period may be launched by one multiparty coalition government in a state and approved by another combination of parties in power at the Centre. However, shortly thereafter, there may be a change in the government in the state and/or at the Centre. With every such change in the government at the

Centre, there will be a change in the composition of the earlier Planning Commission (which is now the NITI Aayog [also known as National Institution for Transforming India]). The same is true at the state level: There is a realignment of the political relationship between the parties in power at the Centre and in different states with a change in government. Governments are political bodies and their decisions are discretionary. Thus, it is likely that each year, the actual flow of central assistance to different states will be increasingly determined by the timings of elections and the party composition of the coalition governments at the Centre and the party or parties in power in different states.

So far, by and large, India has been exceedingly fortunate in having persons of calibre, integrity and patriotism in top leadership positions, irrespective of the nature of the coalitions to which they belong. However, it cannot be taken for granted that this situation will continue indefinitely in the future. While the country still has the good fortune of having highly distinguished leaders at the helm, immediate action needs to be taken on two fronts.

First, more financial powers and increased responsibility for the implementation of development programmes should be entrusted to the states. This is not because all states are likely to be more scrupulous or consistent in the exercise of their powers, but because greater transparency and competition among states would, at least, ensure that the better governed states have easier access to financial resources and the opportunity to implement their programmes.

Just as the Finance Commission is constitutionally empowered to decide on the division of tax resources between the Centre and the states, a similar federal commission should be statutorily set up to decide on the devolution of all other forms of central assistance. The allocation of non-tax central assistance should be related exclusively to the implementation of approved anti-poverty and development programmes in physical terms. The greater the success of a state in implementing a programme in relation to its target in quantitative terms, the higher should be the allocation of central funds to that state.

Second, all appointments in autonomous institutions, regulatory bodies, public enterprises, banks and financial, educational and cultural institutions in the public sector should be entrusted to specialized bodies set up along the same lines as the Union Public Service Commission (UPSC). These bodies should follow transparent procedures for recommending appointments to the top positions. Their recommendations should be invariably accepted by the government (as is the case with UPSC recommendations for entry into the civil services and other appointments under its purview). Similar procedures, at an arm's length from the government, may be adopted for top appointments in the services. Recent developments and the controversies surrounding them in many of India's top institutions, highlight the need for urgent action to insulate public institutions from excessive political interference in their day-to-day work.

The Council of States

In respect of elections to the Council of States (i.e. the Rajya Sabha), the Representation of the People's Act, 1951, was amended by the Parliament in August 2003. The two significant amendments were: (i) persons elected as members of the Rajya Sabha do not have to be residents of the states that elect them; and (ii) the secret voting procedure, which is applicable in all other elections, has been replaced by open voting. A dissenting member who votes against a party candidate is likely to be removed from his or her party as well as from the state legislature for indiscipline and defection.

At first glance, the above two amendments appear quite reasonable. It is a well-known fact that in the past some members who were not ordinarily residents of a state, had declared themselves to be residents of that state in order to qualify for elections to the Rajya Sabha. Similarly, it has also been noticed that some electors in state legislatures had voted in favour of candidates belonging to other parties in exchange for financial and other favours.

In practice, however, the combined effect of the above two amendments has had a substantial impact on the composition of the Rajya Sabha and made the so-called Upper House of the Parliament even less representative of people than was the case in the past. Neither the people of a state directly, nor their representatives in the state legislature indirectly, have any voice or discretion in electing their representatives to the Rajya Sabha. The choice of members now depends entirely and exclusively on the leaders of various parties. Anyone with sufficient resources, organized manpower and access to leaders can be elected from anywhere, depending on the ability of a party to swing sufficient number of votes in the state legislature. A system of quid pro quo among the parties has also developed where one party can provide balancing support to another party in one state in exchange for similar support by that party in another state.

The Rajya Sabha, over a period of time, is also likely to become a safe haven for leaders who fail to get elected to the Lok Sabha. Public-spirited individuals and those with a background of service to the people of a particular state will still get elected as nominees of different parties but, over time, such cases are likely to become fewer in number. Taking into account the working of our system of parliamentary democracy with more than fifty parties being represented in state legislatures and the Parliament, there is no doubt that, eventually, the composition of the Rajya Sabha would become vastly different from what was envisaged in the original Constitution.

A reform of the present system for elections to the Rajya Sabha is now urgent. In case it is not politically feasible to reform the electoral process, it would be much better for the functioning of our democracy to have a unicameral Parliament, as is already the case in some states. This will not only save time and budgetary resources, but will also prevent further erosion in the federal character of the Indian Union.

One argument against having a unicameral legislature is that it may affect the quality of the Cabinet. This may happen in case some prominent and qualified persons belonging to a political party (which is called to form the government) happen to lose the Lok Sabha elections or are not inclined to contest elections. At present, they can be elected to the Rajya Sabha and are able to find places in the Cabinet, if their party so desires. The same is true of some highly qualified persons from different professions, industry and trade.

These concerns are valid. It is in the larger public interest for the prime minister to be able to appoint the most qualified persons in the country to the Cabinet. However, this objective can be achieved by adopting a constitutional amendment to the effect that a majority government can, if it so wishes, appoint, say, up to 25 per cent of the members of the Cabinet from outside the Parliament. Those who are appointed in this manner may be authorized to participate fully in the proceedings of the Lok Sabha in their ministerial capacity, without having the right to vote. Interestingly, this is precisely the case now in respect of members of the Rajya Sabha, who are appointed to the Cabinet.

State Funding of Elections

The issue of the State funding of elections has been considered from time to time in the Parliament and other forums. However, so far, no consensus has emerged, even though there is a general agreement that the need to collect large funds for elections is a primary cause of political corruption. It is also a known fact that, over time, while large amounts are being raised in the name of political parties, a substantial portion of such funds are being diverted for personal use. The print and electronic media have exposed several high-profile cases of the accumulation of illicit wealth by chief ministers, ministers and other leaders in and out of office.

It is obvious that given the large number of persons with criminal records who are active in politics, state funding of elections will not eliminate corruption entirely. However, it would at least help those who want to remain in politics without having to indulge in corruption. State funding may also help in reducing the acceptability of corruption as an unavoidable fact of Indian political life and strengthen NGOs or other individuals in the fight against corruption.

One argument which is frequently advanced against state funding is that it would favour large parties and would, therefore, be unfair to small or new parties. Another argument is that the fiscal cost of such funding will be high and unbearable for many states as well as the Centre. While there is indeed some merit in both arguments, they are, by no means, persuasive and compelling.

To take the second argument first: The size of the Budget expenditure by the central government is estimated to be more than ₹20 lakh crore for financing the Lok Sabha elections and providing some support to state governments for the state elections. Even if such elections are held twice in every five years (because of greater political instability), this amount should be sufficient to provide adequate funds for legitimate electoral expenses in each Lok Sabha constituency. In terms of the central Budget, the amount to be earmarked for elections could, thus, vary from 0.2 to 0.4 per cent of total expenditure annually (depending on the frequency of elections). By no means can this be regarded as an unbearable fiscal burden for a cause as vital as election funding.

It may also be mentioned that the central government allocates nearly ₹3,500 crore annually to fund the Members of Parliament Local Area Development Scheme (MPLADS). State governments have similar schemes for their Members of the Legislative Assemblies (MLAs). In view of the significant misuse of such allocations, as highlighted by the media from time to time (which has led to the expulsion of several Members of Parliament [MPs]), it is desirable to discontinue MPLADS-type schemes both at the Centre and in the states. From the country's point of view, it would be much better if budgetary funds allocated for such schemes were used for election funding.

It is also feasible to introduce a practical scheme for the equitable distribution of electoral funds among large and small political parties. The proposed distribution formula, given below, is by no means perfect, but it should broadly meet the legitimate concerns of small parties:

- Funds for elections to recognized political parties should be provided under two broad heads: (a) to reimburse certain categories of identified election expenditure; and (b) to meet a relatively small amount of residual expenditure on staff and maintenance of party election offices.

- A predetermined category of actual expenditure, which should be eligible for reimbursement, could cover newspaper and television advertising for a specified period, say, two or three weeks prior to elections and reasonable transport costs by air and train for election campaigns. Rules for reimbursement of actual expenses under these (and any other admissible heads) may be laid down by the Election Commission of India (EC). Advertising by political parties may be limited to the amount which is eligible for reimbursement. In other words, parties which benefit from state funding for advertising, should not be allowed to spend any additional amount under this head, on their own account. They can incur additional expenditure on their own, if they wish, on all other items such as transport, staff and offices.
- The division between 'large' and 'small' parties for the purposes of allocation of funds may be made according to a benchmark, approved by the Parliament after appropriate consultations with the EC. Thus, parties with, say, a minimum of 10 or 15 per cent of the seats in the Lok Sabha or the state legislatures (for state elections) may be considered as 'large' parties; the rest can be considered as small parties.
- Reimbursement of actual expenditure under the prescribed heads may be the same for all large parties (as defined by the Parliament for this purpose) and proportionately less for smaller parties (depending on the actual number of seats held by them in the Lok Sabha

or state legislatures).
- Allocation of funds to meet residual expenditure on staff and offices may be weighted by the number of seats held by each party. The weights may be suitably devised to ensure that the larger the party, the higher is its entitlement for funds on this account. At the same time, small parties should not be put to undue disadvantage.

As a large and vibrant democracy, India is not alone in facing the problems of electoral funding through legitimate means. The costs of contesting elections in India and elsewhere have increased phenomenally in recent years because of changes in the methods of communication. In addition to personal campaigning, the use of electronic media for sending messages to voters has become unavoidable in all democracies. While costs have increased and there are several elections to fight every year at different levels (i.e. national, state and district), contributions from reliable sources have dwindled. Fewer persons now become party members or make contributions to political parties. The same is true of charitable organizations and the corporate sector.

In order to overcome these problems, some of the old as well as new democracies, including the United Kingdom (UK) and the US, have introduced some funding of political parties through transparent and verifiable rules. India must do the same as early as possible.

A further step, which deserves urgent consideration, is that of state funding of some additional electoral expenses, as per certain guidelines which are in public interest. This will enable small as well as large political parties to avoid reliance on undeclared donations.

The Budget for 2017–18 announced the following measures

for introducing transparency in electoral funding of political parties through donations by individuals, partnership firms, Hindu Undivided Family, and corporates:

- In accordance with the suggestion made by the EC, the maximum amount of cash donation that a political party can receive will be ₹2,000 from one person.
- Political parties will be entitled to receive donations by cheque or digital mode from their donors.
- As an additional step, the Reserve Bank of India (RBI) Act will be amended to enable the issuance of electoral bonds in accordance with a scheme formulated by the government. Under this scheme, a donor could purchase bonds from authorized banks against cheque and digital payments only. They will be redeemable only in the designated account of a registered political party.
- Every political party would have to file its return within the time prescribed in accordance with the provision of the Income Tax Act.

The above steps are certainly worthwhile, as exemptions to political parties from the payment of income tax would be available only subject to fulfilment of these conditions. At the same time, it is also likely that the above provisions would not be sufficient to meet actual electoral expenses being incurred by most political parties at the Centre as well as states.

Role of Small Parties in the Government

In a democratic State, every citizen has a legitimate right to vote, contest elections and launch a political party. If a party enjoys the minimum electoral support prescribed by the EC, it is recognized as a national or regional party. At the national level, regional parties are also eligible to join a coalition government. Irrespective of the size of their representation in the Parliament, they can continue to function as separate parliamentary parties with their own agenda. In principle, this is a reasonable arrangement in a diverse, multiparty country with a federal constitution like that of India.

An important principle of parliamentary democracy is that the government is formed with the support of a majority of directly elected members in the House of the People (i.e. the Lok Sabha). Each member has a single and equal vote. Once a government is formed, whether by one party or by a number of parties in a coalition, it is supposed to be collectively responsible to the Parliament and, through it, to the people.

Unfortunately, over time, these fundamental principles of parliamentary democracy have been compromised. Small parties, with less than 5 per cent of the national votes and an even smaller number of members in the Parliament, now command a disproportionate influence as partners in a coalition government. Even a collective decision of the Cabinet can be shelved or overturned at the insistence of a supporting regional party. If the coalition government consists of a number of small parties and is also dependent for survival on the support of other parties outside the coalition, then the situation becomes even more complicated. The government may continue in office, but it is unlikely to enjoy sufficient political authority for efficient governance.

Another consequence of the formation of governments with the inside and outside support of a large number of small parties has been political instability, or at least the threat of it. After 1989, as many as six governments were not able to complete their full term. This was also the case in respect of two coalition governments which were briefly in office during the period 1977–79 (after the Emergency of 1975 was lifted). It is also worth recalling that two of the worst economic crises faced by India, in 1979 and 1990, were, in no small measure, due to the inability of governments then in power to take timely corrective action because of uncertainty about their survival in office.

Political uncertainty and instability are sometimes unavoidable in a parliamentary democracy where a large number of parties have conflicting interests. Although we now have a majority party in office, in future, it is important to ensure that all parties that form a coalition, function collectively in order to provide efficient public administration. To this end, it is particularly desirable to reduce the disproportionate power enjoyed by small parties that decide to join a coalition.

At present, a small party is free to join a coalition and hold crucial ministerial berths. It is also free to follow its own regional or sectoral agenda in the exercise of its ministerial responsibility. In case it is dissatisfied with a decision of the Cabinet, it can threaten to walk out of the coalition and reduce the government to a minority. In order to avoid fresh elections, it can continue to support the government from outside if and when a no-confidence motion is moved by the Opposition. In this way, the members of a defecting party can continue in Parliament/legislatures. At the appropriate time, they can also join another coalition.

In order to prevent defections by individuals or groups of members of a party in the Parliament/legislature, in 1985 and again in 2003, the Constitution was amended to disqualify them from continuing as members or holding any other public office until their re-election. A similar measure should be introduced to disqualify members of a party (with say, less than 10 or 15 per cent of seats in the Lok Sabha, as may be decided by the

Parliament), who opt to join a coalition and then decide to defect. It should be made mandatory for all members of such a party to seek re-election.

As provided in the 2003 amendment, members of a defecting party should also not be permitted to hold any public or ministerial offices during the remaining part of the term of Parliament/legislatures. There is no justifiable reason why members of a small party should be put in a more favourable position than any other group of defecting members. Indeed, it can be argued that the present system provides a built-in incentive for the fragmentation of a large party into smaller separate parties at the time of elections. The leader of a small party enjoys all the benefits of being part of a larger party formation (e.g. occupying a ministerial berth) without any of its disadvantages. These rules should also apply to 'independent' members who opt to join a coalition government.

Further, in order to reduce the threat of political instability in the future, it is also desirable to introduce an amendment in the rules of business in the Parliament. It may be provided that all parties in government should become members of the same parliamentary party under the banner of their coalition. They should not be recognized as separate parties for purposes of parliamentary business. Thus, for example, the National Democratic Alliance (NDA) or United Progressive Alliance (UPA) [or any other coalition that forms the government] should be considered as the NDA or the UPA parliamentary party, respectively, as long as it is in office. Such an amendment will have the salutary effect of formally recognizing all parties in a coalition as a joint parliamentary party for conducting the business of government in the Parliament/legislatures. All such parties may, of course, continue to have their separate identity for all other purposes, including the power to nominate their own candidates during elections.

Role of the Parliament

In governments formed by a coalition of parties, the responsibility of the Parliament to enforce the accountability of the multiparty executive has increased, but, unfortunately, its power to do so has diminished. In order to restore the relevance of the Parliament in a parliamentary democracy, it is now imperative to take measures to make its proceedings orderly. There must be strict rules of business, which should not be altered or violated with impunity. A possible approach to achieve this objective could be as follows:

- In theory, the Speaker and the Chairman have the power to expel or suspend a member from the House. But these powers have seldom been exercised. A convention has developed whereby the House can be adjourned several times during the day or for a whole week or more in the event of disruption by a few members. It may be specifically provided, by legislation, that either House of the Parliament cannot be adjourned more than twice in a week unless the listed business, including carried-over business from previous sessions, has been completed after full discussion as per the time allotted by the business advisory committees of the Parliament.
- No bill or legislative business of the government should be approved by a 'voice vote'. It should be made compulsory to adopt all bills after the division and counting of votes. This would require one or two hours of additional time to pass a bill—which is not excessive. If, because of unruly behaviour and disruption by members, a bill cannot be discussed and voted upon, then so be it. In case the matter is considered urgent or there is a national emergency,

the Speaker/Chairman should be empowered to convene a special session, during which no other matter can be raised.

- A legislative provision may be made to the effect that the established rules of procedure for conduct of business of the House cannot be suspended or amended after a session of Parliament has been formally convened, except during a national emergency declared by the government, with the approval of the president. In other words, the ad hoc and sudden suspension of rules of business should not be permitted.
- The Budget and finance bill to be passed only after consideration by the concerned standing committees of the Parliament. This rule, which is already in place, should be made compulsory. If, for any reason (such as election schedules), sufficient time is not available, then only a 'vote-on-account' should be passed by the Parliament.
- The Speaker/Chairman should be required mandatorily to suspend or expel members who frequently disrupt the House. If members from any side of the House (those belonging to ruling parties or the parties in Opposition) disrupt the work of the House on, say, more than two occasions in a week, it should be incumbent on the Speaker/Chairman to continue with the session (by suspending or expelling defaulting members) rather than adjourning the House.

The above rules will, by no means, eliminate all the problems that affect the functioning of the Parliament at present, but will certainly help in making its sessions more purposeful.

Reform of the Government

In India, governments at the Centre and in states, along with their agencies, have, practically, unlimited powers to pass laws, notify rules and regulations and determine economic and social priorities. Some of these may require parliamentary or legislative approval, but as long as a government has the requisite majority, such approval is a formality. While available powers are enormous, it is also a fact that the authority of the government to actually enforce laws and rules is minimal. Part of the reason is, of course, judicial delays.

Several surveys and opinion polls have provided telling statistics about the extent of corruption in government agencies. A survey by the Public Affairs Centre, based in Bengaluru, found that in recent years, every fourth person in one of the large cities in India ends up paying a bribe when dealing with agencies involved in urban development, electricity, municipal services and telephones.

Interestingly, despite the deepening crisis of governance, India is currently witnessing a new growth momentum. This paradox is largely explained by three factors. First, beginning in the early 1980s, the government's heavy-handed control of the non-governmental sectors in manufacturing as well as services, was lifted. A second factor was the gradual opening up of the economy through reduction in protective tariffs and abolition of import and export quotas of various types. India became an attractive global destination for capital, skills and business outsourcing. Finally, particularly after the 1997 Asian crisis, India managed its external sector exceedingly well. After nearly four decades of periodic crises (beginning in 1956), India emerged as a country with a strong balance of payments (BoP) and one of the highest levels of foreign exchange reserves.

It is interesting to note that all the three factors were related to positive changes in macroeconomic policies, which created a more competitive environment, and removed extensive governmental controls over individual and corporate initiatives. These had very little to do with institutional or micro-level changes in the administrative and governance structure within the government.

The fact that the overall rate of growth in the economy has accelerated due to resurgence in the private sector, makes the need for reforms within the government even more urgent. In a poor country with a large population, where the bulk of the people are dependent on agriculture and have access to a few basic amenities, a high rate of growth in the national income by itself cannot reduce disparities or remove poverty. Government intermediation in favour of a more equitable distribution of the benefits of growth through the provision of public services and public investment in basic infrastructure is essential.

Even if we assume that as many as 200–250 million people are currently benefiting from the high rates of growth in manufacturing and services in the private sector, more than 800 million persons in India will still continue to be at the periphery of prosperity for quite some time. Meanwhile, the widening of disparities among different sections of the people can cause severe strains in the political and social life of the country.

The kind of reforms that are required and feasible in the current political scenario is a matter on which there is likely to be vast differences of opinion among experts and others. Let me mention only a few vital principles which, in my view, need to be adopted as early as possible in order to guide the process of reforms in the next few years:

A Definitive Agenda for Political Reforms

- The political role of the government in the economy needs to be redefined and prioritized. At the macroeconomic level, the political (i.e. ministerial) role of the government should be to ensure a stable and competitive environment with a strong external sector and a transparent domestic financial system. While the macroeconomic priorities (for example, the trade-off between growth and inflation) may be decided by the government, the instrumentalities for achieving these objectives must be left to autonomous regulatory and promotional agencies.
- The government's direct role in economic areas must be reset in favour of ensuring the availability of public goods (such as roads or water) and essential services (such as health and education) to the people. In these areas, the government's role must expand substantially. At the same time, its role in managing commercial enterprises deserves to be correspondingly reduced. The latter objective should be achieved without, in any way, affecting the financial and other benefits of those who are presently employed.
- Another important priority is the simplification of administrative procedures and reduction in the number of agencies, at different levels, involved in providing clearances for undertaking any activity. This is an area where the supply of corruption by public servants creates its own demand. Except in selected areas of paramount national interest (such as security and defence), it is desirable to cut through the elaborate red tape and rely primarily on 'self-certification'. The government can lay down standards and norms (for example, in respect of environmental impact or safety) and the entity concerned may be required to 'self-certify' that these have been

complied with as per the notified procedures. Government agencies can make random checks and in case there are violations, appropriate penal action can be taken.

- A related area is transparency in the decision-making process within the government. A major step in this respect has been taken with the enactment of the Right to Information (RTI) Act, 2005. A further step in this direction is to make it mandatory for all ministries and departments of the government to voluntary make information on the decisions taken by them available to the public (excluding security-related subjects). It may be clarified that information should be released by the ministries themselves without the need for any member of the public to ask for it. If this is done, the free media and civil society institutions will constitute an effective instrument for enforcing accountability in the decision-making process itself.

- Case studies of international experience in the management of public services show that the objective of such programmes can be achieved better, and at less cost, if a distinction is made between the ownership of these services (by the government) and the delivery of such services (by NGOs and local enterprises). In such cases, the public authorities retain the responsibility for regulating and monitoring the activities, providing subsidies where necessary and laying down distribution guidelines. In India, a noteworthy example of public-private collaboration in the area of public services is the public call offices, which have revolutionized the availability of telephone services all over the country since 1990s.

Ministerial Responsibility

A minister, as the political head of a ministry, enjoys enormous executive powers. Part of the rationale for entrusting politically appointed ministers, of whom several have very little previous administrative experience, is that the ministry is supposed to be accountable to the Cabinet and the Parliament, through them.

While the above system is sound in principle, in practice, there has been substantial erosion in the ability of the Parliament/legislatures to hold ministers responsible, either collectively or individually, for the decisions taken by them on behalf of their ministries. In addition to the principle of collective responsibility—which shields ministers from taking individual responsibility—another reason why they are not held accountable is that most subjects in economic area, which are of direct interest to the public, are in the Concurrent or State Lists of business.

The central ministers are free to make pronouncements, approve policy guidelines and set all-India targets, but the actual implementation of programmes happens to be in the hands of individual states. A familiar excuse given by central ministers for their failure in meeting the targets announced by them is that the states, and not the Centre, are responsible for the implementation. The states, on the other hand, blame the Centre for inadequate allocation of funds, inappropriate guidelines and approval delays by one or more ministries at the Centre.

Assuming that political parties, civil society and enlightened members of the Indian public are serious about removing the worst forms of poverty and deprivation, a new institutional initiative is urgently required for enforcing ministerial responsibility for the efficient delivery of public services and anti-poverty programmes all over the country. This can be achieved only if the cherished doctrine of collective and concurrent responsibility for all actions of the government is replaced by the notion of individual responsibility of ministers for implementing programmes that they announce. The doctrine of collective responsibility can continue to prevail for all other political purposes, including the continuation of a government in office.

Another area where immediate action is necessary is that of lowering the bar on political corruption. A lid has to be put on the tolerance levels of corruption, at least at the ministerial level. Persons who have been chargesheeted for corruption, fraud and similar criminal offences should not be permitted to take the oath of office and function as ministers until they are cleared by the courts. A special procedure may be set up to immediately hold and expedite court hearings in cases of persons who are proposed to be appointed as ministers.

Depoliticization of Civil Services

A great deal has already been written on the atrophy, non-accountability, corruption and ineptitude of the Indian civil services. In addition to academics and international agencies, this view has been expressed by a number of civil servants who recounted their experiences after their retirement from the highest offices of the State. There is now almost complete unanimity that, despite having some of the best and brightest persons in the civil services, the system as a whole has become relatively non-functional.

The basic issue that needs to be tackled for improving the morale of the civil service is really that of the 'separation of powers', within the executive, between ministers and civil servants—especially in matters concerning postings, transfers and promotions. The separation of powers among the three branches of the government—the executive, the legislature and the judiciary—is already enshrined in the Constitution. Although there has been considerable encroachment of the executive powers into the legislative, and even the judicial areas (and also the other way round), it can still be said that these three separate branches enjoy substantial autonomy and independence. Within the executive branch, however, the civil service is now completely dependent on the pleasure of the ministers in regard to even the most mundane and routine administrative matters. It is essential to revert to a rule-based system of administration, which circumscribes the powers of politicians and confers greater authority on the civil service itself for self-regulation.

Similarly, while economic policy decisions can be taken by the Cabinet or its ministers, specific cases should invariably be decided by permanent administrative committees. They will, of course, be accountable to political authorities and, through them, to the Parliament for the decisions taken by them.

The greater empowerment of the civil service must go hand in hand with the greater accountability of civil servants for their performance and ethical conduct. In view of the time-consuming process of enquiries and judicial delays, the possibility of any penal action being taken for even the most blatant actions of civil servants is considered remote. They may be apprehended and sent to judicial custody for a few days. Thereafter, more often than not, they are released on bail and enjoy complete freedom of action, including the right to contest elections after retirement from the service.

There are two statutory provisions, namely Article 311 of the Constitution and the Official Secrets Act (OSA), 1923, which require reconsideration. Widely misused, Article 311 provides comprehensive constitutional protection for a person holding a 'civil post from being reduced in rank, removed or dismissed from service'. The OSA provides protection to civil servants and ministers from being held accountable for any action that can be labelled as secret by them. The RTI has substantially reduced the power of civil servants to deny information to the public. There is no reason why the OSA should still remain valid.

It may be clarified that the withdrawal of constitutional and special statutory protection provided to civil servants will not, in any way, affect their service conditions, pay and other benefits. These will continue to be determined as per the present rules and procedures.

Fiscal Empowerment

An important step was initiated in 2003, when the Fiscal Responsibility and Budget Management (FRBM) Act was adopted. The objective, as defined in the Act, was to ensure sustainable fiscal management and long-term macroeconomic stability. The FRBM Act was further amended in 2012. The FRBM rules formulated in 2013 provided for a reduction of gross fiscal deficit to 3 per cent by 31 March 2017. The budgets for 2017–18 and 2018–19 have exceeded the target of 3 per cent but deficits are still relatively lower than was the case earlier—the deficit was 3.5 per cent in 2017–18; estimated to be 3.3 per cent in 2018–19. On the whole, there is no doubt that as far as fiscal responsibility is concerned, India has done extremely well compared to most other emerging market economies.

The fundamental issue that requires attention, relates to the present pattern of government expenditures and the use to which resources raised through revenue or fiscal deficits are being put. If the deficits were used productively and could generate a sufficient rate of return to cover the repayment of past debt, the precise level of the deficit—within certain sustainable levels—would not have mattered all that much. Alternatively, if the government's tax and non-tax revenues were in surplus over current expenditure (including subsidies), that surplus could have been used to service past debt. Depending on the level of tolerance for inflationary pressures and the growth rate of domestic savings, a certain amount of revenue or fiscal deficit would also be feasible without giving rise to financial instability and undue pressures on the economy.

In India, over the years, the basic problem has been that the bulk of government expenditure is now devoted to payment of salaries and servicing of past debts. New programmes are launched but governments are fiscally 'disempowered' from carrying them out in time. Despite large deficits, sufficient resources are not available for financing essential capital expenditure, improving public services and undertaking even the routine maintenance of infrastructure. Fiscal disempowerment is not confined to rural areas; even the fastest-growing cities are affected by the government's inability to provide civic amenities.

The same is true of several states in India. According to official statistics, despite sharp increases in resource transfers from the Centre and high revenue deficits, development expenditure, as a proportion of total expenditure of state governments, has actually been declining. It is even more striking that, within the total development expenditure on all accounts, social sector expenditure (comprising social services, food storage, rural development and warehousing) is also likely to show a proportionate decline (along with a rise in population).

In order to improve the economic conditions of the bulk of the country's population and reduce disparities in access to essential services, it is imperative for all states to take urgent measures to fiscally empower themselves. As past experience shows, higher fiscal deficits or larger transfers from the Centre do not provide an adequate solution to the problem of fiscal stringency.

The solution lies in altering the pattern of expenditure away from salaries and loss-making commercial enterprises and allocating larger resources for the development of infrastructure and socially productive sectors. In the Budget for 2018–19, the proposed capital outlay is projected to increase by less than 1 per cent over revised estimate of outlay in 2017–18.

Legal and Judicial Reforms

Judicial delays in India are now legendary. In view of the long delays and multiple levels of appeal available to any person or organization, filing a case has become a convenient way of avoiding a contractual obligation or conviction for a crime. As a result, all courts, particularly high courts, are now overburdened with pending cases.

There are multiple causes for this state of affairs in a vibrant democracy like India. A person is free 'until proven guilty' and the burden of proof lies on the prosecutor. In principle, this is as it should be. Unfortunately, in practice, there are enormous delays at the level of investigating agencies in collecting evidence. Corruption among witnesses and others is also widespread.

An important reason for judicial delays is the plethora of legislative provisions on all aspects of national life, some of which are one hundred years old and internally contradictory. All ministries of government, at the Centre and in states, are keen to introduce fresh legislation and amendments to old statutes

A Definitive Agenda for Political Reforms

every time the Parliament/legislatures meet.

It is also an age-long practice, since the British times, for all bills passed by the Parliament/legislatures to include an omnibus provision that gives unfettered right to the government to notify 'rules' notwithstanding any other provisions of the Act or any other laws in force. The rule-making provision, which has the force of law, provides sufficient scope for the discretionary and arbitrary exercise of power by the executive.

Fortunately, in recent years, four states—Haryana, Punjab, Himachal Pradesh and Kerala—and one union territory—Chandigarh—have successfully taken action to reduce cases pending for over ten years in lower courts to less than 1 per cent of total pendency. Some of these states have also fixed annual targets and action plans for judicial officers to dispose of old and criminal cases where the accused have been in custody for over two years. The future action plans for these states also reveal how high courts are actually improving the process of monitoring pending cases by shifting from a monthly to quarterly review of judicial officers' performance to improve the quality of disposal of such cases.

In the next five years, it would be desirable for the Centre to reform the legal system in all the states to reduce pendency below 1 per cent. To achieve this objective, there is now an urgent need to reduce the scope for appeals, adjournments and frequent hearings at different levels of the judiciary.

The above ten-point programme of political reforms which may be introduced by the government in the next few years is, by no means, exhaustive. The implementation of these programmes would certainly increase political stability, reduce the powers of multiparty coalitions at the Centre as well as in states and help in reducing economic disparities in the long run.

2

Preserving Unity in Diversity in the Parliament

The Parliament of India is truly representative of the vast economic, social, regional and religious diversity of India. All income classes are represented—from the richest industrialist to the poorest farmer. All castes and regions find equitable representation depending on their size, population and electoral popularity. Members belong to different religions and can openly and freely espouse their beliefs, irrespective of their numbers.

In the midst of this great diversity, there is also unity. Every member has a single vote and an equal right to intervene in the debate independently or on behalf of a party. The time and space allotted to a party or non-party members is also equitably distributed, depending on their numbers. Ministers speak on behalf of the government, but have no special privileges inside the House. While there is discussion and debate on important matters, and there are strong political differences among the parties within and outside the government, most legislative proposals and official resolutions are generally adopted without dissent.

While all this is true, below the surface, in recent years, there has been a subtle change in the role of the Parliament. All citizens who follow the news or who watch Parliamentary proceedings are aware of, and perhaps disappointed by, the frequent disruptions that now occur in the two Houses. Several years ago, the concern with the functioning of India's Parliament and state legislatures was also voiced by the NCRWC:

> If there is a sense of unease with the way the Parliament and the state legislatures are functioning, it may be due to a decline in recent years in both the quantity and quality of work done by them. Over the years the number of days on which the houses sit to transact legislative and other business has come down very significantly. Even the relatively fewer days on which the houses meet are often marked by unseemly incidents, including use of force to intimidate opponents, shouting and shutting out of debate and discussion resulting in frequent adjournments. There is increasing concern about the decline of Parliament, falling standards of debate, erosion of the moral authority and prestige of the supreme tribune of the people.[2]

In the context of coalition politics, there is also increasing acceptance by political leaders of the frequent violation of democratic norms and conventions in the political decision-making process. As a result, there has been a possible threat to the preservation of the cherished goals of 'Unity in Diversity' since the early years of the country's freedom. Some signs of an increasing divide in the national mainstream are already evident.

---

[2]Report of the National Commission to review the working of the Constitution. 2002. Government of India.

In several states, lawlessness has spread in a large number of districts. Political leadership has been ineffective and there have been frequent and arbitrary transfers of senior police officials and other district officials. The duality of India is also evident by the increasing income disparities among the people, seen in the vast contrast between India's rising global economic clout (as reflected in the large number of Indians on the list of the world's billionaires) and the deteriorating conditions in its rural areas, where a majority of its citizens live. This divide is also reflected in the divisiveness at the highest levels of the government, where ministers and leaders belonging to different parties are inclined to follow their own agenda rather than pursuing a collective and shared vision for the nation's future.

Diminishing the Role of the Parliament

In the annals of India's long and distinguished parliamentary history, the events that took place over five days—between 18 and 22 March—during the Budget session of 2006, were perhaps unique. Over the course of these five days, a number of unexpected decisions were announced by the government regarding the business agenda in the two Houses, which were passively accepted by both. These decisions involved a major change in the established procedure for consideration of the Budget, a drastic revision in the business of the two Houses without adequate notice and the sudden adjournment of the Parliament sine die (followed by a reversal of this decision again a few days later).

The passive and ready acceptance by the Parliament—the supreme institution of India's democracy—of decisions that are contrary to well-established parliamentary conventions, had serious implications for the working of the institution. It is, therefore, worth going into the events of these five days of March, in some detail.

As per the usual procedure, the Budget session of the Parliament was convened by the President to meet in two parts—from 16 to 17 March and again from 3 to 28 April. However, on 7 March, in view of elections announced by the EC in five states over the months of April and May, it was decided to have a longer interval between the two parts. Thus, the dates were revised, and it was decided to hold the first session from 16 February to 22 March, and the second session from 10 to 23 May. Though the first part was longer and the second part was a bit shorter than the original schedule, on the whole, the session was supposed to be long enough to permit the examination of the Budget as per established convention.

It will be recalled that, according to rules 272 and 331G of the Rules of Procedure and Conduct of Business in the Rajya Sabha and the Lok Sabha, respectively, it is mandatory for the demands for grants of the ministries and departments of the government of India to be examined by the concerned standing committees of the Parliament. These standing committees—which were set up in 1993—consist of members of both Houses of the Parliament. The agenda and meetings of the committee are conducted by a chairperson, who is normally a senior member of one of the Houses. The examination of the Budget grants by these committees allows members, belonging to both Houses and different parties, to question the senior representatives of the ministries or departments and also hear and examine other witnesses, including members of NGOs and experts. The observations and recommendations of these committees are normally unanimous and non-partisan. Reports on matters under their purview, including the Budget demands, are submitted to the two Houses of Parliament for consideration.

In order to allow the standing committees sufficient time for careful consideration of the Budget demands, it has also been the convention for the Houses to adjourn for about a fortnight between two parts of the Budget session. The first part of the session is devoted to a general discussion of the Budget by members and the reply by the finance minister on broader macroeconomic aspects. The reports of the standing committees on ministries/departments are considered in the second part of the session followed by voting on the demand for grants and consideration of the finance bill for the new fiscal year.

Coming back to 2006: After the change in the dates was announced, a controversy arose about the definition of the so-called 'office of profit' (OoP). Some members were alleged to have been appointed to such offices by state and central governments, which is not permissible under the Constitution. One well-known MP was also disqualified on these grounds by the President, on the EC's advice. It was in the context of this controversy that a number of decisions were announced by the government and were accepted by the Parliament, which violated several well-established conventions and norms.

Thus, on 18 March 2006, without any prior intimation, the government decided to introduce a motion in the Rajya Sabha for the suspension of Rule 272 (and Rule 331G in the Lok Sabha). The motion to suspend the consideration of Budget demands by the standing committees was moved and adopted without discussion in the two Houses on the same day. With the suspension of consideration by the standing committees, the ground was cleared for the adoption of the Budget as well as the finance bill in the first part of the session itself. This was an extraordinary and unprecedented event in a year which saw no change of government, general election, or internal or external emergency. And yet it was decided to rush the Budget through Parliament without proper consideration.

Rule 272 was suspended in the Rajya Sabha on 18 March and Rule 331G was suspended in the Lok Sabha a day earlier. On 20 March, the consideration of the Budget demand for grants (or the appropriation bill) as passed by the Lok Sabha on 18 March, was listed in the revised list of business in the Rajya Sabha. The controversy on the OoP issue had become more intense because of allegations and counter-allegations by major parties about top party leaders holding various OoPs under the central and state governments, and still continuing as MPs. Nevertheless, the budget appropriations were considered and approved by the House on the same day. On the next day—21 March, a Tuesday— the finance bill, i.e. the bill to change tax laws, was listed in the revised list of business and was duly approved by a voice vote in the midst of considerable noise and disruption.

Developments in the Parliament on 22 March were, however, even more extraordinary and unexpected—and, in some sense, bizarre. Before the Parliament convened in the morning on that day, there was a strong rumour that the ruling coalition was considering exempting certain offices from the purview of the proposed OoP legislation by issuing an ordinance after the first part of the Budget session would end in the evening. The reason for this extraordinary move, as reported in the press, was to ensure the continuation of the then Congress party president's term in the Parliament. At the time, she was also holding the office of chairperson of the National Advisory Council (NAC) with a Cabinet rank. Unfortunately, at the time of her appointment, the government had not taken steps to exempt this office, which could have been done easily and without any controversy.

The opposition parties, as a mark of protest, decided to disrupt the Parliament on 22 March, and did not allow any listed business to be considered (the Union Budget had already been passed the previous day). After an obituary reference, which lasted for about four minutes when the House met, in view of shouting by some members, it was decided by the chairman of the Rajya Sabha to adjourn the House for twenty minutes. The House met as scheduled but was again adjourned after four minutes of disruption and was asked to meet later in the day. However, during those four minutes, more than a hundred papers, including the annual reports of public sector organizations, outcome and performance budgets, 'action taken' reports and the notifications issued by various departments of the government, were laid on the table of the House by a dozen ministers in the midst of the pandemonium.

The House met for the fourth time that day at 2 p.m. and was adjourned after two minutes, for half an hour. Again, there was a disruption and it was adjourned until 5 p.m. The House met for the sixth and last time, at 5 p.m. This last session, which lasted for only fifteen minutes, completed all the listed business for the day, including the adoption of a legislative bill without any discussion, in a noisy and disrupted House.

No explanation was given in the House for the reasons to suspend the Budget session after the first part. However, in response to questions by the media, it was explained by the government that the House had been adjourned sine die because the Budget had already been passed and there was hardly any business left to be transacted.

The end of the Budget session on 22 March was followed by a surprise announcement on the next day—23 March—by the then Congress president. She decided to renounce her seat in the Parliament and seek re-election after resigning from all other government positions (including that of the chairperson of the NAC). According to media reports, in the light of this unexpected development, the government had no option but to give up its plans to issue an ordinance exempting certain offices from the purview of OoP rules. In a subsequent press interview, it was announced by the concerned minister that the government would consult other parties in the Parliament and bring about appropriate legislation for consideration in due course.

After four days of abrupt sine die adjournments, the government announced its intention of reconvening the Parliament, as earlier scheduled, from 10 to 23 May. A formal notice to this effect was also issued to all members on 5 April after the necessary formalities had been completed. On 28 March 2006, members were also informed that related Parliamentary standing committees will examine these demands for grants and present their reports thereon to the respective Houses in due course.

Thus, the standing committees were also resurrected as suddenly as they had been dispensed with—even though there was nothing left for them to consider, recommend or approve. This move was yet another step in the direction of diminishing the role of the Parliament in the conduct of the nation's affairs.

The Parliament now does what the executive decides or does not decide, presumably after some behind-the-scenes consultations with selected party leaders. The events of 18–22 March, and the subsequent decision to reverse some of the unconventional decisions taken earlier, are perhaps a culmination of a process marked by adhocism and expediency in the functioning of the Parliament.

Role of the Opposition

It may be argued that the primary responsibility for the above series of events lies with a disgruntled Opposition and not with the government. It was the Opposition that was indulging in frequent disruptions in the two Houses and the government had no option but to somehow carry on with the task of running the affairs of the nation.

This contention may have some validity, but it does not resolve the issue of complete subservience of the Parliament to the will of the executive. If bills can be passed, if budgets can be approved and if sessions can be adjourned abruptly, an irresponsible or autocratic government in the future can easily get away with the erosion, and even suspension, of the legitimate rights of the people. So far, with one or two possible exceptions, the country has been fortunate in having been led by leaders of integrity and democratic values, despite the ups and downs of coalition politics. However, there is no guarantee that this will continue to be so in the future.

There is also no legitimate explanation for the decision to end the Budget session well in advance of the announced schedule or suspend the procedure for examination of the Budget by the standing committees and then reverse these decisions arbitrarily after a couple of days. The sanctity of well-established conventions and practices deserves to be preserved rather than abandoned on grounds of expediency. This is feasible if the Parliament, rather than the executive in power, is in charge of its own functioning and the chairs of the two Houses are given adequate powers to control an unruly Opposition.

It is the duty of a democratic and elected government, to not only somehow carry on with the business of governance, but also ensure that the means adopted for doing so, conform to the best practices in a democracy and the intent of the Constitution to make the executive accountable to the legislature rather than the other way round.

Silence as Loud as Debates

In addition to approving legislative proposals and other government business, the Parliament is an important forum for the discussion of important public issues and grievances through their representatives. There are regular 'question hours' for members to ask the questions of their choice concerning different ministries. Ministers are responsible for answering these questions and for taking further action as necessary in the light of the discussion on 'starred' questions.

Time is allotted for members to make 'special mentions' on an issue of importance to their constituents, their states and the country. A member is entitled to propose a 'short duration' discussion on any matter of public importance. He or she can also move a resolution or a private member's bill for discussion and approval after completing the necessary formalities for doing so.

Debate on important policy issues is exhaustive, penetrating and highly useful. The issues raised during the debate also influence the course of policy formulation by the government of the day. This is an important strength of India's democracy as long-term national policies of domestic and international importance, including economic policies, are adopted after careful consideration and a broad consensus across the political spectrum. This explains why national policies, once approved by the Parliament after discussion, are seldom reversed despite changes of government.

However, there have been occasions when the silences of the Parliament have been just as loud as the debates on foreign policy, employment and development policy. Generally, the tolerance for deviation from established norms and propriety is most evident when the interests of the leader of the party in power are under threat or there is a clash of interests among different parties in search of political power after elections (or an adverse judicial verdict). The most conspicuous example of such silences was, of course, during the period of the Emergency in 1975–77, when violations of established laws and administrative norms were either tolerated or approved through legislative amendments, including constitutional amendments.

Fortunately, for our democracy, such occasions have been relatively infrequent. The power of the Parliament to alter the fundamental rights of the people and the 'basic structure' of the Constitution has also been declared invalid by the Supreme Court of India as early as 1973—during the hearing on the famous Kesavananda Bharati versus State of Kerala case. The verdict of the Supreme Court in this case was challenged in 1975 by the then government after the imposition of the Emergency. It was argued that the Parliament was 'supreme' and represented the sovereign will of the people.

As such, if the people's representatives in the Parliament decided to change a particular law to curb individual freedom or limit the scope of judicial scrutiny, the judiciary had no right to question whether it was constitutional or not. After listening to the persuasive arguments of legal luminaries like Nani Palkhivala, the then Chief Justice of India decided to dissolve the bench and the 'basic structure' doctrine was reaffirmed as an unalienable feature of our Constitution[3].

The 'basic structure' doctrine has not been challenged or compromised by any party or parties in power after 1975. However, in recent years, the silences of the Parliament have become more frequent on several issues of public interest. New state governments have been sworn in even though they did not have a majority in the legislatures. Ordinances have been issued by governments without adequate cause and prosecution of criminal offenders has been deferred to protect the political interests of some parties or powerful leaders. On such issues of paramount national importance, the Parliament has maintained a stoic silence or given its approval post facto under the Constitution in case such approval was required.

Again, these cases have been exceptions, and despite the silences and tolerance of the Parliament, the wrong decisions taken by constitutional authorities have generally been reversed later, after judicial scrutiny. However, some unhealthy precedents have been set, and it cannot be taken for granted that these will not be repeated in the future. It is useful to remind ourselves of some of the recent cases where the Parliament did not play its part in holding the executive accountable for its actions. The aggrieved persons or parties needed to approach the judiciary for the redressal of their grievances.

The role of state legislatures in defending the provisions of the Constitution, including the procedure for the approval of state Budgets, has become even more perfunctory than that of the Parliament. In some states, the Budget sessions are now held for a few days only and budgets are passed practically without any

---

[3]For details, see Jalan, B. (2008). *India's Politics: A View from the Backbench*. Penguin UK.

discussion. The same is the case in regard to the approval of new laws or legislative amendments proposed by the government. Part of the reason for this state of affairs is the unbridled power of the Opposition to disrupt the House, and the pressures of coalition politics. The greater the chaos generated when the House is in session, the greater the publicity. Such publicity is considered to be a major gain for parties outside the ruling coalition.

Coalitions and the Parliament

There has been a fundamental change in India's democratic politics. Multiparty coalitions, which include post-election allies, were common at the Centre until 2014 and a norm in several states of the Union. This development is accepted by all political parties, including the Congress party which, till then, was in denial. However, the implications of this important change in electoral reality for the effective governance of the country have not yet been fully appreciated.

The frequency of elections and the expectation that the tenure of a new government may be short (with some exceptions from time to time, as is the case presently at the Centre after the 2014 elections), has had several unintended consequences for the functioning of the Parliament and other vital pillars of India's democracy. The power of the leader of a party over its members in the Parliament is supreme and unquestioned, and what happens in the Parliament now is largely determined by the political interests of different parties rather than by the intrinsic merits or demerits of actions taken by the executive.

Most of the smaller parties have a narrow social base, but their leaders enjoy considerable political power in view of their ability to swing relatively small numbers of votes in favour of another party—particularly, in marginal seats. The frequent splits among parties and the tendency among smaller party formations to destabilize governments, have important behavioural implications for coalitions which come to power after elections.

In order to prevent the destabilization of a government by splitting a party that is a part of the ruling coalition and prevent cross-voting during Rajya Sabha elections, two important legislative changes were adopted by the Parliament in April 2003. The first amendment was that any elected member (or a group of members) who decided to leave his or her party would have to seek fresh election. The second amendment (pertaining to election to the Rajya Sabha) replaced secret voting by an open-voting process by MLAs. This amendment was designed to prevent cross-voting so that members who did not vote for their party's candidates could be removed from their party for 'indiscipline'. The domicile requirement of candidates for Rajya Sabha elections was also removed.

On the face of it, these amendments seem sensible because they are designed to reduce instability and corruption among the members of a party. However, in reality, the effect has been to strengthen the powers of party leaders over their members. The solution adopted, with multiparty consensus, is, in fact, a lot worse than the disease.

While members have no right to defect, the leader of a small party is free to create instability by forcing all members of the party to leave the coalition, even if the majority of the members do not agree with that decision. Similarly, nomination to the Rajya Sabha has become the sole prerogative of the leader of a party (and a few persons who enjoy his confidence). Bribery or the funding of parties in exchange for nomination to the Rajya Sabha has also not been curbed. Indeed, in the long run, the new amendment may encourage institutionalized corruption in the nomination process.

While Parliament sessions are held frequently and huge volumes of papers containing information on the working of ministries are placed before it, the frequent disruptions in the working of the Parliament have established, beyond reasonable doubts, that it has practically no role in holding the government accountable for its performance or even deciding when and for how long it will meet to conduct its business. It is now a regular practice for government business or legislative proposals that require parliamentary approval to be approved without much debate and within a few minutes towards the end of the day when only a few members, including those from the parties in power, are present.

There was a time when assurances given by ministers on the floor of the Parliament had a ring of credibility to them. Unlike other commitments, those made in the two Houses were supposed to be translated into reality—if only for the fear of attracting motions of breach of privilege. This is no longer the case. Assurances in the Parliament are now just like any other assurance: meant to be bypassed or forgotten without explanation. Hundreds of assurances—some of them more than a decade old—are still pending. With a higher turnover of ministers, nobody takes any personal responsibility for assurances given by previous ministers.

Another consequence of the expectation that a particular multiparty coalition, which is dependent on the support of a large number of parties, may not last long, is the politicization of civil administration at the Centre, states and districts. Increasingly, with the possibility of only a short duration in ministerial offices, the political leadership, with few honourable exceptions, is inclined to give preference to its party's political, sectional and financial objectives rather than the larger public interest.

The purpose of highlighting the wider implications of multiparty coalitions in the functioning of the Parliament and other areas of governance is not to undermine the legitimacy of coalitions in a democracy. As in several other countries, coalitions are—from time to time—unavoidable in a parliamentary system of government, or for that matter, in a presidential system with a separate legislature.

At the same time, it has to be recognized that if disparate multiparty coalitions have become a regular feature of our governance system, then certain changes in parliamentary procedures are also essential, such as those pertaining to the role of small parties and the system for enforcing accountability of the executive for its decisions. This is particularly important in a country that is characterized by widespread poverty, disparity and deprivation among its people.

It also has to be recognized that the emergence of coalitions as a regular form of multiparty political system was not fully foreseen at the time that our Constitution and the rules of parliamentary procedures were adopted after considerable debate. In the light of emerging requirements and experience, India has, so far, carried out more than a hundred amendments in its original Constitution and several changes to its electoral and legislative procedures. If some more amendments are now necessary to accommodate the realities of coalition governments as a regular feature of our democracy, they must be undertaken sooner rather than later.

An urgent reform that is required is to introduce amendments to reduce the present built-in incentive for the fragmentation of parties and improve governance. It is of utmost importance that the anti-defection law must be made applicable to all parties and the so-called independent members who choose to join a government in power. In other words, those parties which join a pre-election or post-election coalition should not be able to defect without having to seek re-election. Such an amendment to the 'anti-defection law' will go a long way in strengthening the principle of collective responsibility of the Cabinet to the people, as enshrined in the Indian Constitution.

3

Criminals in Politics

All parties—old and new—nominate some persons with a history of criminal offences or other legal violations, to contest elections. Governments in all states (with perhaps one or two exceptions) have cabinets that include a fair number of such persons in charge of sensitive ministries. In recent years, with the emergence of coalition governments, this is also the case at the Centre. A common defence of this practice is that persons with criminal records have been elected 'by the people'. Therefore, in a government 'of the people', they cannot be denied their just rewards.

Interestingly, at the time of appointment or entry into professions, this argument is not applicable to any other public servant or members of any other profession. An interesting consequence of the special position accorded to criminals in political life is that the 'demand' for entry into politics by those whose cases are pending in judicial courts at different levels, has increased substantially. The 'supply' of offices or constituencies to meet this rising demand has, however, not kept pace.

The organizational structure of political power resembles a pyramid: It is wide at the base or the grass roots, where the number of persons elected to political offices—such as gram panchayats—is large and entry is relatively free; however, the number of such offices shrinks drastically at the district, state and union levels. The size of the electorate increases exponentially as one moves higher up the ladder, while the number of political constituencies and offices reduces. As the level of an office becomes higher, the pyramidal structure of political power increases the mismatch between supply and demand for that office and increases its scarcity value.

This phenomenon partly explains why, at higher political levels, entry into politics has become more and more restrictive. Access to politics at the higher levels (with some honourable exceptions) is now available only to persons with sufficient 'clout', in terms of family connections, money, ethnic and caste loyalty and/or coercive power. Competitive politics has also made electoral politics expensive, which has further reduced its accessibility to the average person who lacks adequate means, power and command over a community's resources.

Another consequence of the high value attached to scarce political power is the emergence of leaders who enjoy a 'monopoly' in the use of power. This explains the virtual disappearance of inner-party democracy from the Indian political scene. Most parties, again with a few exceptions, have leaders who alone (or with the help of some trusted aides) decide who will fight elections, who will join the Cabinet and who will get nominated to various political and government offices. In case there is a threat to the power of a leader from another aspiring member of the same party, s/he is likely to be expelled or declared persona non grata. Alternatively, if that aspiring member has adequate political strength and following, the original party is likely to split. Parties may also split up from time to time for other reasons—such as joining a coalition in power or accepting the inducement offered by an aspirant with money or clout. As a result, the number of parties vigorously contesting elections shows a secular increase over time, with most parties winning only a few seats.

As one moves up the political pyramid, the 'scope' of power available to leaders also increases, further enhancing the scarcity value of power and demand for such offices at higher levels. At the village level, the principal responsibilities entrusted to political representatives are relatively few—such as the identification of beneficiaries under poverty alleviation and employment generation schemes, distribution of subsidized agricultural inputs, local infrastructure projects and miscellaneous welfare schemes (old-age assistance, disaster relief and housing programmes for the poor). However, they have very little budgetary or financial powers to raise resources, and the bulk of fiscal resources for poverty alleviation programmes are allocated by the central and state governments.

The scope of powers available to political leaders increases enormously at the state and central levels. At the state level, in addition to a hundred or more centrally sponsored and state poverty alleviation and other schemes, there is a large number of infrastructure projects under management or construction. Another important source of financial power is the state cooperative banking structure with its district and primary cooperative societies, which are fully or largely under the control of political representatives.

In addition, there are numerous public sector commercial or service organizations that have been set up by state governments and are directly under the control of political leaders in administrative ministries. State governments also have practically unlimited powers to establish new agencies and public sector organizations, with separate budgets and management structures.

At the Centre, of course, the entire governance machinery of the country, the predominant proportion of fiscal powers (including exclusive jurisdiction over custom tariffs and corporate taxation), the large public sector undertakings in important sectors of the economy (such as banking, insurance, petroleum, food procurement and food distribution) and control over allocation of national resources (including investment in crucial sectors such as power, roads, aviation and ports) are under the control and direction of political leaders. All matters relating to defence and external affairs, including defence procurement, are the exclusive preserve of the central government.

Dominance of Criminals

Persons with long-standing criminal records have been free to contest elections and assume political office because technically, as per the law, they are presumed to be 'innocent until proven guilty'. In view of lengthy legal procedures and multiple levels of appeal, persons charged with committing even the most heinous and grave offences can remain free and continue to contest elections over an indefinite period.

Political power provides additional protection against conviction for past offences because of control over government agencies responsible for investigation and prosecution. There is a natural reluctance among investigating agencies and government ministries to speed up the investigation and prosecution of persons who are leaders of political parties and/or members of the Cabinet. According to the statistical survey of elections to the Lok Sabha in recent elections, cutting across party lines, it was found that nearly 20 per cent of the candidates (excluding independent ones) had criminal antecedents. In the present Lok Sabha, which has 543 seats in all, well over a hundred members, elected in 2014, had criminal cases pending against them.

At the state level, the dominance of criminals varies from state to state. Some have a lower proportion of criminal candidates, while many have a substantially larger proportion of criminals as candidates than at the Centre. Recently, the National Election Watch (NEW) and Association for Democratic Reforms (ADR) analysed the self-sworn affidavits of 4,823 candidates out of 4,853 candidates who contested in the 2017 assembly elections.[4] Out of 4,823 candidates, 859 (18 per cent) had declared criminal cases against themselves of which as many as 704 candidates had declared criminal cases related to attempt to murder, kidnapping, culpable homicide, communal disharmony, electoral violations and crimes against women, among others. Of these, sixty-two candidates had declared cases related to murder under Section 302 of the Indian Penal Code.

The ADR also analysed the self-sworn affidavits of 402 out of 403 newly elected MLAs. It was found out that as many as 143 (36 per cent) MLAs had declared criminal cases against themselves. Among these, 107 (26 per cent) MLAs had declared serious criminal cases, including cases related to murder, attempt to murder, etc. This is significantly higher than the number of MLAs who had declared similar serious criminal cases against themselves in 2012.

In view of the choice of a political career by persons with a criminal past, it is often said that in India and some other democracies, a person would rather be in politics than in jail. The

---

[4]Reports for Uttar Pradesh | Association for Democratic Reforms. (n.d.). Retrieved from https://adrindia.org/research-and-reports/state-assemblies/uttar-pradesh

ease with which individuals with known records of corruption and other crimes are selected by political parties to contest elections partly explains the low esteem in which politicians are generally held by the public in India.

An important reason for criminals being elected to the Parliament and legislatures is the high cost of contesting elections. In a multi-tier democracy like ours, all citizens are free to fight elections either on behalf of a political party or as independents. Elections are held at different times at various levels of the political structure. In the era of coalition governments, elections at the state and central levels have also become more frequent than was the case earlier.

Political leaders are, therefore, virtually in campaign mode during most of the year, on behalf of themselves or other candidates nominated by their parties. In view of India's large population, at the higher levels of the political system, the constituencies are also large—indeed larger than those found in any other established democracy in Europe, Asia or America. Although the size of the constituencies across the country varies greatly—depending on the geography and population density—on an average, the number of voters in a constituency for elections to the Lok Sabha is more than 1 million people, spread over a large geographical area. In the electronic age, the cost of campaigning for elected office is also high, particularly for the publicity, transport and subsistence of political workers.

State Funding of Elections

In order to make elections affordable and accessible to parties or individuals who do not have very large funds, the EC has put limits on the maximum expenditure by a candidate in a constituency.

There are also prescribed rules for political parties to declare their assets as well as the contributions that they may receive. These rules have laudable objectives. However, in practice, they have had some perverse results. The rules are scrupulously adhered to on paper, but there is strong evidence that actual campaign expenditure has not been contained. Excess expenditure over the prescribed limits is being financed through two other sources: (a) supply of free campaign goods and services directly by unnamed contributors; and (b) financial contributions to the party or to candidates in cash and 'undeclared' funds.

However, as it happens, the actual expenditure can easily exceed these limits without any problem. Thus, Explanation 1, Section 77(1) of the Representation of the People Act, 1951[5], allows political parties and their supporters to spend any amount in a given constituency—over and above the expenditure ceilings applicable to individual candidates—provided there is no direct coordination with, or mention of, the candidates. This legal loophole permits any candidate to spend indirectly as much as s/he wishes through another person or political party.

The need to raise large funds for financing elections has made political corruption widely acceptable and unavoidable in most constituencies across the country. There are, of course, some exceptions. Persons with a high political standing, popularity or personal wealth do not necessarily have to rely on undeclared sources of funds to fight and win elections. However, in most parties, such persons are in a small minority. To make corruption a less compelling factor in the need to raise funds for elections, it is now imperative for India to introduce a fair and equitable scheme for the state funding of elections.

---

[5]http://eci.nic.in/eci_main/CurrentElections/ECI_Instructions/ins_290307.pdf

Compulsions and Pressures of Power

The procedure for elections to the Rajya Sabha was radically changed in 2003 by amending the Representation of the People Act, 1951, in both Houses of the Parliament. The domicile requirement for a candidate to be elected from a particular state was removed and the provision for secret ballot by members of state legislatures was replaced by open voting. Thus, a person, residing anywhere in India, can now be elected to the Rajya Sabha from any state. If a party has the requisite number of votes in the legislature to elect a member to the Rajya Sabha, the members of that legislature have no option but to vote for the party's candidate.

The amendments in the election rules were justified by the then ruling coalition on the ground that some elected members were, in any case, making false declarations about their domicile in a particular state and that the earlier provisions for secret ballot were encouraging cross-voting by members for wrong reasons—such as bribes. Unfortunately, irrespective of the intentions underlying these amendments, the actual effect has been to strengthen the grip of a few leaders in deciding who should represent a particular state in one of the highest forums of India's federal democracy.

So far, many of the candidates selected for elections to the Rajya Sabha by different parties have impressive credentials. At the same time, there is also evidence that any person with sufficient resources and/or personal clout can find a berth in the Rajya Sabha with support from one or more parties from some state or the other, even if s/he has no connection with that state.

The amendments to the rules for election to the Rajya Sabha have, no doubt, curbed the scope for corrupt practices by a few individual members of a state assembly. Unfortunately, in practice, these amendments have also caused immense damage to the reputation of an August House of the Parliament in the public mind. All electoral powers of the Rajya Sabha are now concentrated in the hands of the leaders of political parties; some of whom, as widely reported in the media, are inclined to use these powers to raise additional funds for themselves or their parties from aspiring candidates.

As is well known, MPs and MLAs enjoy various perquisites such as housing, free travel and constituency allowance, in addition to a basic salary. In a large country like India, where most of the legislators are not permanent residents of Delhi or other state capitals, there is perhaps a good case to be made for providing such facilities. The scale of facilities available to a member, however, increases dramatically when he or she becomes a minister in the government or a holder of any other high public office. Ostentatious displays of power as a VIP and VVIP have become an essential part of the perquisites of an office holder in a democracy which, many years ago, was established on the principles of simplicity and sacrifice by the representatives of the people.

Conspicuous consumption, high living and ostentation by the so-called 'public servants' could be dismissed as frivolous and unworthy of serious comment but for the fact that these have had the most unfortunate effect on party politics. The sense of deprivation and loss of social status in losing office—and all the paraphernalia and manpower associated with it—among members of a party, have important behavioural implications for all political parties, particularly the small regional ones.

In India, family ties also play a strong role in determining a person's position in the social hierarchy. As such, the sense of deprivation affects not only those who participate in politics directly, but also all those who are associated or connected with them. The compulsions and pressures to remain in power are, therefore, enormous. This partly explains why political parties are quick to change sides or split into small formations in the event of a threat to the stability of a coalition government.

No wonder then that physical scuffles and assaults among some members of small parties with members of parties that are in power in state assemblies and even in the Parliament, are not an uncommon sight when tempers rise because of charges of corruption and wrong-doing by leaders of one political party or another.

The present incentive for persons who have criminal cases pending in higher courts of appeal (either a high court or the Supreme Court) should be effectively reversed by giving such cases the highest priority if the concerned person is actually elected to the Parliament or a state legislature. Their 'presumed' innocence should be proved within six months of election before they can take their seats in the assembly or the Parliament. Fast settlement of such cases would provide a big relief to persons with criminal charges who are actually innocent and not only 'presumed' to be so. On the other hand, those who are actually guilty may choose not to contest elections so that they are in a position to delay hearings through normal legal procedures.

4

Corruption Multiplier

As is well known, despite several positive actions taken by present and earlier governments to reduce the level of corruption in the administrative and political system, India continues to have one of the worst rankings in the Corruption Perceptions Index and Global Corruption Barometer compiled by Transparency International. In the latest index for 2016, India's score was 40 on a scale of 0–100, where 0 is supposed to be 'totally corrupt' and 100 'very clean'. This is better than India's score of 38 in 2014 and 2015, but it indicates that corruption is still very high. There is no doubt that the existing level continues to pose a serious threat to the security, freedom and well-being of ordinary citizens and their cherished democratic values.

Towards Zero Tolerance of Corruption

In 2013, an important step was taken by the then government to reduce the level of corruption in India: A bill was introduced in the Parliament to amend the Prevention of Corruption Act, 1988. The purpose of the bill was to replace the earlier definition of criminal misconduct. It provides that the intention to acquire assets disproportionate to income should also be proved, in addition to possession of such assets. However, the bill does not cover circumstances where the public official: (i) uses illegal means; (ii) abuses his/her position; or (iii) disregards public interest and obtains a valuable thing or reward for him/herself or another person. Under the Act, the guilt of the person is presumed in respect of offences of taking a bribe, being a habitual offender or abetting an offence. This bill is still pending in the Parliament.

In 2017, the government announced some further measures to reduce the prevalence of corruption in the administrative system and has committed itself to its policy of zero tolerance of corruption in the future. Among the steps announced by the government—some of which were also introduced in the previous years—are the further strengthening of the RTI Act, inclusion of integrity pact in major purchases, ratification of the United Nations Convention against Corruption, placing information on assets of government officers in the public domain, setting-up of additional special Central Bureau of Investigation courts and introduction of e-governance and direct benefit schemes.

A Special Investigation Team has also been formed to detect black money, and foreign travels of government officials on public money have been reduced. The government has also finalized draft rules to put a time limit for each stage of the enquiries to ensure an expeditious disposal of corruption cases. In principle, it has been decided that as far as feasible, the enquiring authority on such cases should conclude the proceedings and submit its report within a maximum period of one year—preferably within six months.

The primary challenge for the government is to successfully implement the measures announced, and to reduce the powers available to officials and different ministries of the government to actually implement these measures on the ground. In this context, it may be mentioned that several of these measures, such as the RTI, were also announced by previous governments during 2004–14.

The primary reason for the slow progress in reducing the level of corruption, despite several announcements, is simply that there is reluctance to reduce the role of government and its organizational structure at multiple levels in the governance and functioning of the economy. It is also generally not appreciated that the adverse effect of high corruption on the country's income, fiscal balance and investment is a 'multiple' of the amount of actual illicit monetary benefit to the corrupt.

An interesting finding of empirical research is that for every rupee of monetary gain to the corrupt, the aggregate loss to the society could be as high as ₹3 or 4. Let us call it the 'corruption multiplier'. Just as money supply in the economy is a multiple of actual money created by a central bank (the so-called 'money multiplier'), there is a corruption multiplier which occurs because of a wrong choice of public projects, loss of tax revenues, low quality of goods and services by corrupt procedures and frequent breakdown of equipment (for example, in power plants).

The worst effect of the corruption multiplier is on total factor productivity and delays in the completion of public projects, particularly infrastructure projects. As it is, government procedures for the approval and financing of investment projects involve a large number of ministries and agencies at the Centre and states, at different levels of administration. If there is corruption at any stage of approval, then the corruption multiplier gathers momentum, and total investment, because of delays, declines by a multiple of actual money transferred to the corrupt.

Supply and Demand of Corruption

The most repugnant aspect of corruption in India is not that it is there, or that it is so pervasive, but that it is widely accepted as an unavoidable feature of Indian life. At the political level, corruption among parties and politicians is believed to be unavoidable as elections have become expensive and funds have to be raised, by whatever means, to contest them. Similarly, in defence of the high incidence of bureaucratic corruption, it is argued that civil servants in India are not paid well or that such corruption is a 'universal phenomenon'.

Large and small corporates in India also choose to survive and thrive by participating actively in corruption on the ground that it is the only way to get their business done. Interestingly, corruption in businesses in India is perhaps as internal (that is, between a private buyer and a private seller or financier) as it is external (that is, between a private firm and the government). The common man or woman also has to participate in corruption because there is simply no other option if s/he has to get a ration card, licence, permission or registration.

In addition to its wide acceptance as a necessary evil, another area of grave concern is the interlocking or 'vertical integration' of corruption at various levels of the government hierarchy—elected politicians; higher and lower bureaucracy. The normal assumption, that the principals at each of the higher levels would be committed to ensure that their subordinates would act according to probity, is no longer valid. In a situation in which principals and agents collude with each other in corruption, the problem of tackling it becomes much more intractable.

Further, there is also a horizontal spread of corruption to other public institutions, including legislatures, parts of the judiciary, media as well as independent professions. This has made the prevention and control of corruption even more difficult. As if all this were not enough, another unfortunate development in recent years has been the politicization of corruption. Increasingly, cases of corruption are being given a political colour without any serious intent to tackle the problem. This has facilitated the entry, into politics, of persons with a track record of corruption. The public no longer knows whom to trust: the accuser or the accused.

Corruption is a major hurdle in growth, development and poverty alleviation. Research has established that it reduces productivity, lowers investment, causes fiscal drain and has a debilitating effect on efficiency. Sadly, these adverse effects are not generally recognized by India's political and legal institutions or even its public. This chapter aims to bring together the available information regarding the ill-effects of corruption on public welfare and the country's economic potential. A related purpose is to suggest measures that can reduce the extent of corruption and its widespread social acceptance by eliminating the causes that give rise to it. Both the demand and the supply of corruption need to be reduced by redefining the role of the State and improving its governance structure.

Economic Effects of Corruption

Until recently, the economic effects of corruption were seldom discussed in the literature on development economics. The reason for this neglect was, partly, respect for the sovereignty of independent developing countries, and partly, because of the difficulty of defining and measuring corruption in a statistically relevant way. In the last few years however, there has been an explosion of interest among researchers in the empirical and quantitative analysis of the effects of corruption on investment, growth and public finances.

Most of this research has originated in international financial institutions, particularly the World Bank and the International Monetary Fund (IMF). These institutions have been involved in financing development and structural adjustment programmes in developing countries for more than five decades. However, these programmes seldom yielded the kind of positive economic results that were initially expected. Over a period of time, it became apparent that part of the reason was the high incidence of corruption. Investment choices are often driven by their potential for corruption and illicit gains rather than their contribution to the national output or the real rate of return on projects. In addition to a strong political bias in favour of launching unproductive and high-cost projects in uneconomic locations, there is also an inherent bias against spending on human capital formation. These activities generally have lower scope for illegitimate monetary transfers to intermediaries.

It is obvious that corruption has a significant negative impact on the ratio of investment to national income and that an improvement in the corruption index (that is, reduction in corruption) can significantly increase the investment ratio and enhance growth. The reason why corruption has a debilitating effect on investment and growth is not only the illegal and clandestine transfer of funds from one set of persons to another, but also the investment choice. Thus, high corruption is often associated with the wrong choice of public projects and project delays, leading to low productivity, low fiscal revenues, low maintenance expenditure and low quality of essential public infrastructure, which, in turn, increases the cost of production of goods and services by business enterprises.

This phenomenon and the negative circular relationship between corruption and investment explain the 'poverty trap' in which many low-income countries, including India, find themselves. This also presents an important dilemma for public policy and development strategy. In countries with poor infrastructure, particularly in rural areas with a high incidence of poverty, public investment is the essential instrument through which productivity and income levels can be raised. At the same time, the higher the level of public investment in relation to GDP, the higher will be the level of corruption and its negative effects on growth in countries with an already high rate of corruption. The solution, thus, becomes the problem. The only way in which this conundrum can be resolved is by taking administrative measures to break the nexus between investment and corruption.

An interesting finding of empirical research is that the adverse economic effect of corruption is more pronounced on small enterprises and the overall growth of employment in the economy. Thus, a survey of 3,000 enterprises across twenty transition economies, covering all regions, found that corruption and anti-competitive practices were perceived as the most difficult obstacles by start-up firms[6]. For large enterprises, corruption often increases profits as it allows them to enjoy monopoly rents and scale economies. For small enterprises, it raises costs and reduces profits because they have to make payments that do not contribute to productivity or output but are necessary for their survival. In order to avoid undue harassment, bribes—which may amount to a substantial portion of the operating costs of such enterprises—have to be paid to meet the demands of a host of

---

[6]'Transition report 1999: Ten years of transition'. European Bank for Reconstruction and Development.

inspectors working in concert with each other. This becomes an important cause of the sickness of small industries, requiring further assistance from local governments or banks, which, in turn, affects their viability.

Since India's independence, central and state governments, in addition to giving various incentives to promote small enterprises, have also launched various anti-poverty rural development and special employment programmes (such as the National Food for Work Programme) to directly benefit the poor and the disadvantaged. Most of the benefits of these programmes are also appropriated by bureaucrats and middlemen at various levels of the administrative hierarchy. Thus, in a memorable and widely quoted observation, Prime Minister Rajiv Gandhi, after visiting some of these programmes, had pointed out that, 'Out of ₹100 crore allocated to an anti-poverty project, I know that only ₹15 crore reaches the people. The remainder is gobbled up by middlemen, power brokers, contractors and the corrupt.'[7]

In fact, the poor are the worst affected by widespread corruption in the delivery of healthcare and other essential public services. In order to enhance the scope for corruption, government expenditures are inflated and wasteful projects and programmes are taken up, including the purchase of spurious drugs and unsafe equipment causing hazards to safety, life and longevity.

While those who are better-off, have access to private providers of essential services, the poor have to necessarily rely on public agencies. They are, however, unable to pay bribes in

---

[7]Badhwar, I. (1989, November 30). Rajiv's campaign trail: Frantic pace | IndiaToday. Retrieved from https://www.indiatoday.in/magazine/cover-story/story/19891130-rajiv-gandhi-campaign-has-a-blistering-pace-but-a-tired-mechanical-air-816789-1989-11-30

order to obtain even the minimum benefits to which they are entitled. Thus, another economic effect of corruption is that it further aggravates inequality in an already unequal society.

As is well known, in order to improve the public delivery of essential services to the poor, India implemented a countrywide experiment with decentralization in local governments after the passage of the 73rd and 74th constitutional amendments in the early 1990s. While the scale and scope of this reform is impressive, the actual working of the decentralized system in different states has revealed a wide disparity. As is well known, in most states, only a limited extent of autonomy has been awarded to panchayats. In particular, education and healthcare—two vital services for the poor—remain entirely outside the province of panchayati authority. There is almost no devolution of unconditional grants to gram panchayats.

The authority devolved to the panchayats concerns the selection of local beneficiaries of government programmes, and the management and implementation of local infrastructure projects covering roads, irrigation and housing. As fund allocation at the district level is grossly insufficient to cover all eligible beneficiaries, corruption and political favouritism at the panchayat level in some states have become routine. This has further accentuated inequality even among the relatively poorer sections of the village population. Kerala is among the few states where levels of participation by citizens in local decision-making on the use of public resources for healthcare and education are significant, and where the level of corruption in the distribution of benefits to the poor is relatively low.[8]

---

[8]Mathew, G., & Nayak, R. C. (1996). Panchayats at work: what it means for the oppressed? *Economic and Political Weekly*, 1765–1771.

Corruption is also an important cause of fiscal drain and higher inflation in developing societies. Countries with high levels of corruption tend to have lower collection of tax revenues in relation to their national incomes. Corruption also has a significant negative correlation with receipts from personal income taxes, since private negotiations with tax inspectors is a common practice in many developing countries, including India.

Indirect tax collections, particularly revenue from custom duties and excise duties, are also highly sensitive to the degree of corruption. It has also been found that higher the level of duties and greater the variability in tax rates (depending on the type of goods), higher will be the scope for corruption and the accompanying revenue drain. As rates increase and corruption rises, the tax system as a whole, becomes less progressive.

In addition to a rise in fiscal deficit and lower progressivity of the tax system, the quality of government expenditure also suffers. The selection of investment programmes, including anti-poverty projects, tends to be guided more by scope for graft and the potential supply of corruption rather than their intrinsic costs and benefits. While elaborate procedures have been set up for tendering and open bidding, much of the mischief is done at the time of specifying the technical details of projects or programmes, which are so drafted as to ensure that the preferred contractors and suppliers are put at an advantage.

For these as well as other reasons (particularly, the preponderance of non-productive revenue expenditure), a high fiscal deficit does not necessarily lead to higher investment or higher output. Despite persistent and high fiscal deficits over the past two decades, capital formation in the public sector in India has been low and declining, with adverse effects on growth.

Thus, contrary to popular perception, corruption is a major

cause of economic backwardness, low growth, high incidence of poverty and fiscal crisis in developing countries. Further, according to surveys, the Corruption Perceptions Index is also higher in countries where the structure and quantity of overall investments were determined by a central planning system, and which had lower per capita incomes and slow progress on structural reforms. These variables alone account for substantial variations in the corruption rankings of countries. Not surprisingly, India ranks high on all three variables as well as on the corruption index.

Anti-corruption Strategies

An effective anti-corruption strategy would need to focus on institutional reform as well as effective measures which reduce both the 'demand' and 'supply' of corruption. There are multiple investigating and prosecution agencies at the Centre and in the states to fight corruption and convict the guilty. Yet, the legal provisions and judicial processes are so cumbersome that cases of successful prosecution of corrupt civil servants or politicians are negligible.

Institutional reform to reduce the number of agencies involved in the anti-corruption drive, along with legal reform, is now essential to provide swift and deterrent punishment to the corrupt. The supply side of the corruption equation can only be checked if there is a substantial reduction in the size and functions of the government, and greater accountability of public servants for the discharge of their duties.

Penalties for corruption, including dismissal from service, have to be swift, so that they have a deterrent effect on the entire civil service and reduce incentives for corrupt behaviour. On the demand side, it is necessary to provide access to scarce public services, occupation and resources through transparent, non-discretionary procedures and market-related mechanisms. Similarly, administrative regulations and documentation requirements have to be substantially scaled down. Measures for institutional reform as well as the 'supply side' and 'demand side' anti-corruption measures are discussed below.

Need for institutional reform

While the number of agencies involved in collecting information, conducting searches and taking the necessary action to bring civil servants and politicians to book have multiplied over time, the quantity of corruption as well as the impunity with which it can be carried out has also expanded. Although the judiciary has passed severe edicts against the executive authority in corruption disputes, in most cases of importance, the investigation either remains incomplete or the evidence is considered weak.

There are multiple causes for the relative ineffectiveness of our judicial system in checking the incidence of corruption or the disposal of even the most outrageous cases of corruption. These have been analysed in considerable detail by a number of committees, including the High Court Arrears Committees of 1949, 1972 and 1990, as well as several Law Commission reports. However, despite much soul-searching, debate and recommendations emanating from these high-level committees, the position of the disposal of cases has not improved significantly so far. Recently, the Supreme Court announced its intention to diminish delays substantially over the next few years. This is a welcome step; however, it is not yet clear if this decision will actually be implemented soon.

An essential component of an anti-corruption strategy for the future is to reduce and revamp the number of agencies and institutions involved in the investigation and prosecution of corruption cases. In any case, no new agency should be set up for this purpose. At the Centre as well as state level, there should be only one specialized agency for the investigation and prosecution of large-value corruption cases against public servants, political representatives and ministers. The cases referred to it should be of significant importance in terms of value, national security or criminal conduct (such as fraud and smuggling). Not more than a handful of major cases should be referred to it, and it should have sufficient access to funds and technical expertise to launch prosecution within ninety days of receiving a major complaint.

The objective should be to provide deterrence and exemplary punishment in a few cases, rather than try and tackle a multitude of cases, which cannot be done effectively. All other cases of corruption should be handled departmentally through an established and transparent procedure, with the help of outside specialized and non-governmental investigative agencies.

Supply-side measures

First and foremost, on the supply side, measures have to be taken to reduce the protection provided to government servants and other public servants under the Constitution and various judicial pronouncements. Most of the constitutional and statutory provisions were intended to provide reasonable security of tenure to civil servants, avoid arbitrary penal action and ensure that due process is followed in processing specific cases. However, over a period of time, the legal framework has become largely non-functional and has been used to provide protection to organized corruption in government and public sector enterprises. Even if there is sufficient evidence warranting dismissal from service, the necessary court orders—after several appeals—usually come through only after the official has retired from service!

Two statutory provisions, among several others, which deserve to be amended, are: Article 311 of the Constitution of India and the OSA. Originally, Article 311 was intended to provide constitutional safeguards for a person holding a 'civil post from being reduced in rank, removed or dismissed from service'. These safeguards were supposed to apply only to government servants—those directly employed by the government at the Centre or in the states under any of the services. They were not supposed to apply to other 'public servants'—those employed by public sector enterprises or parastatal organizations. However, subsequent judicial pronouncements, for all practical purposes, have removed the distinction between the two. This was done through an expansive interpretation of Articles 14 and 16 of the Constitution which incorporate the principle of 'natural justice' as a fundamental right of the people of India.

The provisions of the OSA are so comprehensive that almost all information of the government can qualify to be classified as an official secret. Interestingly, nowhere have the words 'secret' or 'official secret' been precisely defined in the Act, and any kind of information can attract prosecution under the provisions of the Act—whatever the purpose or the impact. This Act and its wide ambit have provided comprehensive opportunities to officials and ministers to cover up their decisions to increase the supply of corruption, in addition to denying the public the benefit of vital information regarding government activities. Decisions can be taken, which are contrary to facts as contained in the relevant files, judicial pronouncements, business rules or previous decisions of interest to the public. The secrecy surrounding the reasons for decisions taken, particularly those which have financial implications, makes it difficult, if not impossible, to detect cases of manifest corruption in time. The incentive for corrupt practices, in secrecy, has increased substantially with a corresponding increase in political instability at the Centre and in several states.

The OSA deserves to be amended as early as possible. The amendment should incorporate a precise definition of what is considered a 'secret'. It should also confine the scope of secrecy to matters of national security and market-sensitive financial information—which should, in turn, also be defined and confined to as few in number as possible. It may also be required that before a file is marked 'secret', a designated high official of the ministry should certify the reasons for doing so. In view of entrenched bureaucratic and political interests, a reform of the OSA is not going to be easy. However, if the supply of corruption has to be curbed, this can no longer be avoided.

A related measure to diminish the supply of political corruption is to reduce the immense powers available to ministers in the decision-making process of a government in office. The fact that ministers are politically responsible to the Parliament/legislatures has led to a situation where practically all decisions, including bureaucratic appointments and postings, require ministerial approval. Policy decisions on economic issues, and rules framed under them, are also so devised as to require a case-by-case approval.

There is no reason why the postings of permanent civil servants, other than those on the personal staff of ministers, should require ministerial approval. Approval by civil service boards, as per the rules already in place, should be more than sufficient for this purpose. Similarly, while economic policy decisions can be taken by the Cabinet or ministers, specific cases should invariably be decided by permanent administrative committees. They will, of course, be accountable to political authorities and, through them, to the Parliament for decisions taken by them.

In countries with low corruption levels, transparency in the decision-making process and full disclosure of decisions taken in financial matters are the most powerful forms of ensuring accountability. Thus, it should be made mandatory for all ministers and departments of the Indian government to make information on the decisions taken by them, available to the public—particularly on matters that have financial implications (excluding purely administrative or security related subjects). The information should be released frequently, after allowing for a time lag where market-sensitive decisions are concerned. This information should be released by the ministries themselves, without the need for any member of the public to ask for it.

India is fortunate that it has a free and vibrant media and strong civil society organizations (including NGOs, business associations, academia and think tanks). The free media and civil society institutions will constitute an effective deterrent to corruption; provided that information on decisions taken by the government is available.

However, there is one important area where the supply of corruption creates its own demand. If administrative rules and regulations are complex and involve multiple agencies acting at cross purposes, then the public has no option but to purchase the required permits, licences and registrations by paying bribes. India's administrative system, despite some recent reforms, continues to be among the most cumbersome in the world, where the public is completely at the mercy of the civil service for getting even the most ordinary permissions (such as a driving licence or the registration of land/real estate). Some measures which are necessary to reduce the demand for corruption are considered below.

Demand-side measures

The demand for corruption has two components. The most pervasive and 'retail' component consists of the demand generated by members of the public who require various kinds of permissions or licences which are necessary to carry on with the ordinary business of life.

The other component is a 'wholesale' one, which is selective and generated by a few corporates (including some large business houses) to take advantage of a restrictive practice or price control for their own pecuniary benefit. This component was most conspicuous during the industrial licencing and control era, when there were numerous controls on output, distribution and pricing. With the liberalization of the economy and the abolition of various kinds of licencing and pricing controls in the 1990s, the demand for wholesale corruption of this kind has reduced, but not yet been eliminated. There is still a long way to go.

While the policies for licencing, price controls, imports and distribution were liberalized in the 1990s, at the Centre as well as in several states, the number of clearances required for setting up industrial plants—and the agencies involved in giving such clearances—have, in fact, increased. The demand for 'wholesale' corruption, despite economic reforms, therefore, continues to be strong.

Thus, for example, in order to set up a medium-size industrial factory, at least fifteen clearances from the state government and six or seven clearances from the central government are likely to be required. Among some of the approvals required at the state level are: site clearance, land acquisition, fire safety, environmental impact assessment and consent, forest clearance, rehabilitation and resettlement plan, power connection, water, consent for road connection to the plant, mining clearance and so on.

In addition, central government approval is also likely to be required for environment, mining, fuel linkage, forest conservation, railway dispatches and conformity with safety or quality standards specified by the central bureaus or ministries. Each clearance is likely to involve more than one government agency and several departments. To expedite clearances or overcome legitimate objections, corruption becomes unavoidable and is considered a necessary component of doing business in India.

◆

After the reform process was initiated in the 1980s, and accelerated in the 1990s, there has been considerable debate in the country on the economic merits and demerits of liberalization and the reduction in the role of the State in the allocation of capital. Much of this debate has been in terms of an optimal or theoretically valid paradigm and ideology: Is liberalization theoretically superior to government intervention? Is globalization consistent with national sovereignty? Is reform of the public sector consistent with public interest in providing services? And so on.

This debate misses an important reason for the adverse effects of excessive State intervention: It increases the incidence of corruption in the economic life of the country. Liberalization of production, distribution and pricing of goods and services, in addition to its positive effects on output, may also reduce the demand for corruption; provided policy liberalization is accompanied by procedural simplification and reduction in the number of clearances required and agencies involved in certifying adherence to multiple legal requirements.

Redefining the role of the State, simplification of administrative procedures and creating a more competitive environment in the economy are essential elements of the strategy for reducing the demand for corruption. However, it must be emphasized that the need to redefine the role of the State in the context of economic reforms does not mean a lesser role for the government or for public policy in widening opportunities and creating a positive environment for equitable development.

In developing countries such as India, with massive illiteracy and underdevelopment of infrastructure, the government must continue to have a crucial role in creating the necessary conditions for growth, through investments in areas such as education, healthcare, water supply, irrigation and infrastructure. Successful economic reforms must result in strengthening the ability of governments to do what they need to do by helping to generate higher growth, higher revenue and higher productivity.

An important measure to reduce the scope of corruption is to decentralize and outsource the implementation of some government schemes, for the benefit of the people, to NGOs or other such agencies on contractual basis. Since the outsourcing and decentralization of such services are likely to be distributed among a large number of organizations—subject to accountability and public satisfaction—there will be a significant reduction in the scope for corrupt practices.

These kinds of reforms can be introduced without causing any harm to the interests of the staff of the relevant departments. They should be provided security of their existing tenures and a generous option for early retirement, so that the surplus staff can be usefully deployed in other parts of the concerned organization, if required. On the whole, the benefits of these reforms to the public and the government are likely to far outweigh the costs.

There is no doubt that an effective anti-corruption strategy covering institutional reforms as well as the supply and demand sides will substantially improve governance and the public delivery system in India. The resulting public confidence and trust in the government, its political leadership and administration, will also strengthen democracy. A byproduct of reduction in corruption due to economic reforms and the redefining of the role of the State in the economy will be an enhancement in the growth rate, productivity and revenues. These, in turn, will enable the government to further accelerate public investment in important sectors such as infrastructure and primary education.

5

Enhancing the Quality of Life

In the past couple of years, the government has taken some important initiatives to accelerate the pace of poverty alleviation in India by making the transfer of subsidies less cumbersome. The two major initiatives include: Direct Benefit Transfers (DBT) and the Pradhan Mantri Jan-Dhan Yojana. These two initiatives are intended to provide cash transfers to the poor in respect of several subsidy schemes. In addition, the recent initiative to launch the GST across all states will also help in the delivery of social services to the people. An important priority for the future is to implement the schemes that have already been announced and spread them all across the country, including rural and semi-urban areas, as early as feasible.

As is well known, the most important measure of socio-economic programmes in a developing country is its rank in the HDI, which is computed annually by the UNDP. The HDI consists of three basic components of human development: Life Expectancy, Literacy and Standard of Living. It is believed to be a more comprehensive measure of progress of a country than the per capita income or growth rate of GDP. In the Human Development Report 2016, India's HDI was 0.624, with a rank of 131 out of 188 countries. India's rank places it in the category of medium human development countries. Though India is currently among the fastest-growing economies in the world, its rank in terms of human development is still relatively low—lower than that of other BRICS countries (**B**razil, **R**ussia, **I**ndia, **C**hina and **S**outh Africa). In the post-2015 development agenda, India is committed to achieving the Sustainable Development Goals, set by the UN, which attempt to address a comprehensive set of socio-economic goals, closely intertwined with improvement in the HDI.

The persistence and depth of poverty in India during the colonial period has been recorded in some detail by economic historians. In the second half of the nineteenth century and first half of the twentieth century, poverty took the form of a series of famines which ravaged all parts of India and resulted in the deaths of more than 30 million people. Epidemics and diseases were also common, and at the time of Independence, an average Indian could expect to live for barely thirty-two years. There was no system of water supply in villages and the supply of electricity in rural areas was unknown. The vast majority of Indians had no access to education or employment. Per capita availability of food actually declined during the forty years prior to Independence by as much as 29 per cent during 1911 to 1941.

After Independence, an overriding priority of the national government, as it has been of all governments since then, was to expand physical facilities to provide basic social services like education, health and nutrition to all sections of the people, particularly the poor. Over the years, the physical infrastructure, in terms of schools, primary health centres and other facilities, has expanded enormously and a variety of social and anti-poverty programmes have been introduced. An effort has also been made to improve the design of these programmes in the light of experience and to make social policies more responsive to the needs of the poor. There is also no doubt that the access of the poor to social services has improved enormously after Independence and an average Indian is significantly better off than he or she was earlier. However, a number of studies and field surveys have also revealed significant weaknesses in the implementation of several of these programmes. Despite the weakness of statistical data, one finding which stands out is that the poor generally have lower access to public social services than the not-so-poor sections of society. For example:

- Despite substantial expansion of the PDS for food, and increase in the availability of foodgrains, the proportion of the population whose income is not sufficient to buy the recommended daily level of intake has remained close to 40 per cent.
- The poor educational and economic background of parents is a major cause of children dropping out from schools. The incidence of illiteracy among the poor, as a result, continues to be considerably higher than the national average in both urban and rural areas. Public schools in poor urban areas are generally worse-equipped in terms of basic facilities (e.g. drinking water) or number of teachers.
- In the case of social assistance schemes like old-age pension and assistance to widows, the identification of beneficiaries has been influenced by considerations other than poverty and the non-poor seem to have benefited more than the poor.

- Owing to the paucity of resources, most social programmes are too thinly spread and fragmented to meet the needs of the poor. Bureaucratic functioning and the social distance of government officials from the really poor are further impediments.

In this context, given the large base of the poor in India, it is obvious that people's access to social services, and the poor's access in particular, cannot be improved without increasing social expenditure substantially over time. There is certainly scope for improving the efficiency of social programmes. Much more needs to be done to target these programmes better, and reduce the weight of the bureaucracy. However, such improvements will not alter the current picture significantly, unless the reach of these programmes is expanded. When public services are scarce and free, they are likely to be pre-empted by the non-poor. In view of fiscal stringency, expenditure on social services in real terms has, in fact, fallen in several states since the second half of the 1980s. It is an important priority now to strengthen the financial position of governments and accelerate revenue-generating economic activity in order to make a breakthrough in the poverty situation.

Important Principles

In addition to the need to increase social expenditures, there are three general principles which should be observed in the organization of social services for the poor. First, there is a need to 'prioritize'. Most developing countries tend to allocate a higher proportion of their meagre resources to provide services which benefit relatively few. Thus, for example, in several developing countries, including India, more is spent on higher education than on primary education. Similarly, more resources are devoted to running specialty hospitals than to, say, overcoming vitamin and mineral malnutrition among the millions of poor.

All countries need facilities for higher education and for specialized treatment of diseases, which also deserve public support. The issue, though, is one of the relative proportion of resources devoted to meeting competing ends. It is not equitable for the government to provide subsidies to cover the entire cost of expensive services for a few people. As a principle, all such publicly supported facilities should be encouraged to cover at least part of their revenue expenditure through charges and fees (with appropriate waivers for those who are not able to pay). In any case, subsidies should be transparent and explicit. The cost of these subsidies should be calculated in per capita terms and periodically published for the information of the public. Quite a number of such subsidies are unconscionably high for a poor country like ours. If there had been sufficient awareness of these costs, they would not have been allowed to continue for so long. A certain measure of self-reliance would also be good for institutions, many of which are now suffering badly for want of adequate budgetary support.

A second principle which should be applicable for all services, including those meant for the poor, is the levy of a reasonable fee which can be waived by the local provider of these services in cases where beneficiaries are unable to pay. There is some evidence that in fee-paying institutions—provided that facilities are adequate—those who can afford to pay are, in fact, willing to pay. Even partial cost-recovery in this manner will improve the quality of services without discriminating against the poor. An alternative scheme, which is now being tried out in some industrial and developing countries is to give vouchers to poor families for certain services, which can be used to pay for these services at any public or private facility that accepts them. The providers of services are encouraged to levy charges which cover their full costs, but they have to compete for clients on the strength of their services. The public cost of supporting these services is reduced, as vouchers are given only to poor families by local authorities. Such a scheme also deserves to be tried out on a pilot basis in India.

There is now sufficient international experience, including in India, to show that involvement of local NGOs in the provision of basic services for the poor can improve their availability as well as quality. NGOs are already active in several fields, particularly education. A number of them, including those in the field of healthcare, have also earned an international reputation for their effectiveness (e.g. the Self Employed Women's Association in Gujarat and the Comprehensive Rural Health Project in Maharashtra). These and other NGOs were able to achieve considerable improvement, at lower cost, in providing basic services to the poor. Their main advantages were a higher level of motivation and the elimination of indifferent government officials from the process of delivery. Central and state governments would do well to channel as much of their social expenditure as possible through local NGOs. The NGOs should be subject to financial and performance audit periodically, the results of which should be published locally.

It is imperative to understand important issues in respect of three priority areas of great social and economic importance i.e. food, literacy and health.

Food security

From an economic point of view, there is nothing more vital than adequate availability of food. The supply and price of food is also directly linked to the issue of poverty in India. The poor spend the bulk of their income on food, and an increase in its price or a reduction in its availability immediately raises the poverty ratio. Food is also a major factor in determining the course of inflation in the economy. It accounts for more than 50 per cent of the Consumer Price Index (CPI). As wages of government and public sector employees as well as employees in the organized private sector are linked to the CPI, the trend in the price of food directly affects the fiscal and broader economic outlook in the country. For all these reasons, self-sufficiency in food production and active intervention in the market for food have been important elements of India's agricultural policy since the mid-1960s.

In the area of food security, distribution of food is as important as its production. Economist Amartya Sen, in his seminal work on famines, showed that these have often occurred when there was little or no decline in food supply (e.g., the Ethiopian famine in 1973 and the Bangladeshi famine in 1974)[9]. On the other hand, despite sharp reductions in food supply, India was able to avoid famines in the drought years of 1965–66, 1973, 1979, 1987 and later, because of effective food distribution policies. These measures made it possible for the affected sections of the population to have access to food despite overall scarcity. The PDS organized through fair price shops and public procurement of foodgrains played a vital role in ensuring access.

A legitimate criticism of the PDS is that its reach has been largely confined to urban areas. Except in times of emergency or drought, the poor in several rural areas are dependent on

---

[9] Sen. A., *Poverty and famines: An essay on entitlement and deprivation*. Oxford University Press, 1981.

private markets for meeting their requirements of food. Food prices in rural markets are often higher, and the government's procurement operations, although necessary and desirable, put further pressure on the rates. In recent years, efforts have been made to 'revamp' the PDS and extend its coverage to tribal, hill and arid areas. This has corrected the urban bias of the PDS, but its coverage still remains regionally uneven. In several states with large concentrations of poverty, the amount consumed by the poor from the PDS is relatively low.

In the foreseeable future, until such time as the dependence of food production on the monsoon is reduced, India will, no doubt, need to continue with the policy of holding sizeable stocks of foodgrains. However, in the light of changes that have taken place in recent years in the cost of holding stocks and other parameters, there is a strong case for substantially reducing the average level of buffer stocks held by the government. In recent years, procurement, distribution and holding costs have risen sharply, partly because of a rise in interest costs and partly because of the 'dis-economics' associated with the large scale of public operations in the area of foodgrains. As procurement prices have become more attractive and more grains are offered to public agencies during the immediate post-harvest period, the peak marketing period is becoming shorter and market arrivals are becoming increasingly concentrated. The problems and inefficiencies in transportation, handling and storage have increased, and so have costs. As a result, the difference between the issue price of grains and the all-in cost to public distribution agencies has widened to a point where the actual benefit to the consumer from food subsidy is substantially less than the fiscal cost of providing this subsidy. The higher the level of average buffer stocks, the lower is the benefit per rupee of subsidy to the consumer.

Another important development that took place recently is the rise in India's foreign exchange reserves, which makes it possible for us to import food from world markets in times of necessity without depending on the goodwill of other countries or institutions. India should explore the possibility of entering into long-term options and contracts which guarantee availability of specified quantities of food at prices which are determined according to an agreed formula. These options and contracts are themselves tradable, so that actual imports and exports can take place depending on the state of domestic production.

Food security must remain an important objective of national policy. India's management of the food economy has paid dividends in the form of higher production, increased access to food and avoidance of famines even during severe droughts. The challenge of the future is to widen the reach of the PDS among the poor and make it more cost-effective and equitable.

Education for all

Development literature, over several decades after India's independence, generally ignored the importance of education and training as factors in promoting economic growth. It was believed that physical capital was crucial for economic growth, and that countries which encouraged capital formation in machines and plants were likely to grow more rapidly.

Since the 1980s, theoretical and empirical research has, in contrast, given prime importance to education and literacy—particularly among women—as key factors in explaining differences in economic performance among developing countries. Cross-country comparisons have indicated that a substantial proportion of the rate of growth of an economy could be attributed to increases in educational levels of the labour force.

While there are differing explanations of the precise ways in which education affects growth, it is generally believed that there are important externalities associated with education, which increase productivity of labour and enhance the rate of technological change in the economy as a whole.

At the time of Independence, it is estimated that about 15 per cent of our population was literate and only one child out of three was enrolled in primary school. Since then, there has been significant progress in increasing literacy rates and expanding the reach of the elementary education system. Literacy rates have increased from 18 per cent in 1951 to a little over 74 per cent in 2015. This record is impressive in view of the pathetically low initial levels of literacy. Over time, the spread of literacy becomes easier as the average population becomes more literate and the incidence of illiteracy among adults and parents decreases.

In order to achieve the goal of universal literacy in the foreseeable future, it would be useful to increase the level of financial support provided by the Centre, for elementary education. It is striking that the per capita incomes of states with a large concentration of illiteracy are well below the national average. In view of the large volume of committed expenditure, the capacity of poorer states to raise sufficient resources for elementary education, even after allowing for a restructuring of public expenditure patterns, is likely to be relatively limited in the near future. The central government should be prepared to finance a portion of the cost of district-level programmes for the spread of literacy, based on past performance and the commitment of individual state governments to eradicating illiteracy.

Equitable access to health services

From a public policy point of view, a principal issue in healthcare is that of equity. The question of equitable access to publicly financed healthcare facilities assumes particular importance in poor, developing countries in view of the inadequate availability of services, high per capita cost and severe limitation of resources. The experience of most developing countries is that access to public health services is largely confined to better-off sections of people in urban areas. Similarly, most developing countries tend to spend more on curative care in expensive hospitals with a limited number of beds, than on preventive care. Expenditure on preventive care is believed to be more cost-effective as the per capita cost of providing such care is generally very low.

Adequate funding is a necessary, but not sufficient, condition for the delivery of health services to the poor. The organization and institutional structure of health services in India suffers from myriad problems, some of which are unavoidable in a country of India's size and diversity. Widespread poverty, illiteracy, lack of rural infrastructure (e.g. roads and housing) and scarcity of trained medical personnel who are willing to work in rural areas constitute formidable obstacles to the organization of cost-effective and high quality health services. Nevertheless, there are some problems that can be resolved in the light of past experience in organizing health services on a large scale.

Recently, in March 2017, the Union Cabinet took a vital decision to introduce a new national health policy, in consultation with state governments and other stake holders, which aims to reform the health system in several ways. An important measure announced in the new policy is to substantially increase the budgeted expenditure on health services to 2.5 per cent of the GDP by 2025, from 1.1 per cent currently. The policy lays stress on the prevention of diseases, instead of just taking care of the sick. The new policy also recommends mechanisms for the speedy resolution of disputes and establishing a National Healthcare Standards Organization to develop evidence-based standard guidelines for care.

These are certainly excellent initiatives to improve the delivery of health services to the poor. At the same time, our past experience shows that the on ground implementation and proper organization of an announced policy is of utmost importance if the goals set by the new policy have to be realized. In the past also, for example in 2002, similar measures to increase health expenditure to 2 per cent and improve its distribution among the poor were announced, but not sufficiently executed. The actual expenditure remained stagnant—around 1.1 per cent of the GDP—since 2002.

In addition to increasing actual expenditure for the poor, it is of utmost importance that certain organizational reforms should also be introduced to improve the delivery system for healthcare. One such reform that deserves to be implemented is to decentralize the delivery of government health services. Decentralization is potentially the most important force for improving efficiency and responding to local health conditions and demands. In India, while local authorities have been given significant authority in some states for managerial services and implementing national programmes, they have practically no financial authority (except in some large cities). Transfers from state to local authorities, for the expenditure on programmes, are also very limited. The bulk of these are 'specific purpose' transfers to cover fixed expenditure, like staff salaries.

The centralization of financial powers is a major hurdle in making health services more responsive to local conditions and local needs. It is also a major cause of delay and inefficiency as even the slightest deviation in the specification of drugs or services requires approval from a number of departments with several layers of bureaucracy, at state headquarters. The decentralization of financial powers, with appropriate audit requirements and performance monitoring, can contribute greatly to improving the quality of healthcare in rural areas and strengthening the accountability of local institutions. It should also facilitate greater participation by the community through NGOs in the health sector. Experience shows that the involvement of NGOs at the local level can be an effective instrument for improving public awareness of health programmes and making primary and community health centres more accountable.

◆

On the whole, India's record in improving the socio-economic well-being of her people is relatively lower than what can be achieved in relation to large annual increases in the overall budget expenditure of the Centre and states. It also compares unfavourably with the average performance of developing countries as a whole. Fast-growing developing countries have, of course, done considerably better than the average, and have succeeded in virtually eliminating illiteracy and substantially reducing infant mortality and malnutrition. In improving access and delivery of food and social services to the poor, India faces significant obstacles arising from administrative bottlenecks and financial stringency. In view of the rising burden of public debt and the growth of administrative expenditure, resources available for investment in social sectors have become severely constrained. There is little hope of improvement in socio-economic indicators, unless public expenditure priorities are reconsidered and altered in favour of social sectors. A high economic growth rate should also help in increasing the availability of public resources for investment in social sectors. Further, data for India as well as other developing countries show that, within particular regions and states, the enrolment ratios in respect of elementary education and demand for primary health services increase with the per capita household income. These demand side effects partly explain why faster-growing economies tend to do better in human development than slower ones.

6
A New Paradigm for the Financial Sector

In the last few years, there has been a fundamental change in the way we think about the financial system and its role in development. Part of this change is due to the changing role being assigned to the government and public sector in the allocation of the nation's savings for development. A bigger reason, however, is the East Asian crisis of 1997. This crisis and its aftermath have brought to the fore, the critical role of the financial system in determining the stability and sustainability of the real economy. As a result, the reform of the financial system and the rules and codes that should govern the conduct of financial business, figure high on the domestic agenda for reform as well as the international agenda for global cooperation.

Valuable Lessons from the East Asian Crisis

Much has been said and written about the causes of the East Asian crisis and its aftermath. The literature is voluminous, and in some ways, it is as impressive as the earlier literature on the 'Asian miracle'[10], and raises the obvious question of what developing countries must learn from their successes. The purpose is not to review this literature, nor to comment on what went wrong and what policies could have been handled in a better way, either before or after the crisis. The purpose here is limited and confined to recapturing some aspects of the East Asian crisis which may have a bearing on our understanding of the relationship between finance and development, and the lessons that countries like India need to keep in view, in order to avoid going through similar devastating experiences in the future.

An important point to remember in this connection is that even relatively small mistakes in the conduct of macroeconomic or exchange rate policies can sometimes lead to big crises. The Asian experience is certainly mixed, and the magnitude of macroeconomic and other policy failures in different East Asian countries was not the same. However, in several of them, the degree of deviation from the best practices or prudent policies was relatively small. It may be that they persisted with the defence of the pegged exchange rates for a week or two longer than was desirable, or it may be that they did not take corrective monetary or fiscal action early enough. However, the devastation and pain that their economies went through because of these policy mistakes were sizeable and unprecedented.

Incidentally, this was also the experience of Mexico and Argentina in early 1995, when a major emerging crisis was brought under a semblance of control by a massive international rescue effort launched by the IMF, the US and the World Bank. It is no coincidence that in all these cases—in East Asia as well as in

---

[10]See Chapter 17. Jalan, B. (2012). *Emerging India: Economics, Politics, and Reforms.* Penguin Books India.

Mexico and Argentina—the proximate cause was the relatively sudden reversal of capital flows on which these economies had become excessively dependent. It had taken a relatively long time to build a climate of confidence, and for capital inflows to rise gradually. However, it took no time for this confidence to be dissipated and for foreign capital to disappear. It is also interesting to note that the major reversal was not only on account of foreign lenders or investors, but also on account of resident holders of domestic assets who rushed to encash or convert their holdings into foreign currency.

The point is simply that handling capital flows is not an easy matter. While capital account liberalization and large capital movements have brought considerable growth benefits, they have also brought with them greater potential for volatility in asset prices and financial markets, including foreign exchange markets. This can cause unanticipated damage to the real economy during periods of uncertainty about the future economic or political outlook. Often, adverse expectations about a country's future during periods of uncertainty can also become 'self-fulfilling'. The fact that such volatility can be aggravated by a weak financial system, leading to severe development problems, should also be borne in mind. The lesson from the Mexican or East Asian episodes is not an argument against capital flows or capital account convertibility. It is about careful and judicious handling of such flows and about the pace of movement towards capital account liberalization for residents. It is also about building domestic safety nets, for example, by keeping the level of liquid foreign exchange reserves high, in relation to short-term external obligations.

It cannot be denied that, despite their earlier spectacular successes, the financial systems of East Asian countries were characterized by several weaknesses. Thus, banks were not subject to effective prudential regulation and supervision. Credit expansion in these countries was large, and banks took untenable positions in real estate and other unproductive assets; in the process, building up large asset-liability and currency mismatches. Banks had also built up huge off-balance-sheet liabilities, which moved on to the balance sheet once there was adversity. Cross-border, inter-bank positions were also large. Non-banking financial companies (NBFCs) contributed to the crisis as they were subject to little or no regulation.

Corporates were also highly leveraged. External debt was available at low interest rates and the fixed exchange rates in these countries offered them a false sense of complacency, encouraging them to hold large unhedged positions. External debt was high, short-term and concentrated in the private sector. Thus, on the whole, there was an inherent vulnerability in the financial sector; and once expectation turned adverse, this vulnerability translated itself into panic. There was also lack of transparency in the operations of market participants as well as the central banks in some cases.

Events in East Asia certainly highlighted the two-way interaction between the financial sector and development, and the need for an appropriate policy framework. Improving the efficiency of the financial sector through market-based reforms is an important concern of the new development paradigm. However, this has to be accompanied by policies, practices and certain amounts of restraint that strengthen the financial system towards stability, so that growth becomes sustainable. At the same time, proper emphasis has to be placed on growth policies that do not give rise to problems that result in a systemic instability in the financial sector (e.g. a large fiscal deficit).

A related issue is that of striking an appropriate balance between financial regulation and market freedom. While freedom is essential to foster efficiency, it also raises an equally important question regarding an appropriate regulatory framework, given the wide divergence between private and social interest in ensuring the stability of the financial system. Hence, a proper system of regulation relating to prudent risk limits, short-term foreign borrowing and the degree of tolerable maturity mismatches in the banking system assumes critical importance for minimizing risks to the stability of the financial system.

The most important lesson emerging from the East Asian crisis was the need to be vigilant about domestic and international developments which could impinge on a country's financial relations with the rest of the world. Over time, the process of integration of worldwide financial markets has resulted in product innovation and efficiency, but it has also made developing countries subject to greater vulnerability and new risks. Strong fundamentals alone cannot provide full immunity from a crisis. There is a need to take early preventive action, build firewalls and keep some safety nets handy. It is also clear that when things are going well, the rest of the world shares in the prosperity. However, when things go wrong, the price has to be paid primarily by the country concerned. It is, therefore, an important responsibility of the countries themselves to put in place an efficient, prudential and safe financial system which can aid and protect the development process at all times—good and bad.

The Indian Experience

Against the backdrop of the lessons from the East Asian crisis, it will be useful to examine issues relating to India from the perspective of our past experience, the present stage of development and policy framework for the future.

The past

As is well known, India's development strategy, for nearly forty years or so after Independence, placed emphasis on State-guided development initiatives, with the primary role assigned to the State and its agencies for mobilization and allocation of savings. It was not until the Eighth Plan that the role of the financial sector and financial markets was given an explicit recognition in the development strategy. The emphasis on accelerating the investment rate through State intervention in a number of key areas, meant channelling credit to certain preferential sectors at subsidized interest rates, exercising public ownership control on most banks and restricting their activities through policy prescriptions. Some of the typical features that got built into this system were the directed lending programme with high levels of cash reserve ratio (CRR) and statutory liquidity ratio (SLR), ceiling on deposit and lending rate, lending to priority sectors, branch licencing and detailed regulation of banks' loan and investment portfolios.

As far as external finance is concerned, India relied primarily on bilateral and multilateral official development assistance and did not encourage private external capital inflows as a way to supplement domestic savings. The exchange rate was administered and there was extensive control over all foreign exchange transactions, which were subject to approval on a case-by-case basis. Because of pervasive exchange controls, the Indian financial system remained largely insulated from international markets. This, however, did not prevent India from suffering regular BoP crises year after year and becoming dependent on aid flows or credits from the IMF.

The financial system, as a result, faced little or no competition—whether domestic or foreign—and costs and efficiency of transactions were not its primary concern. Productivity was generally poor and profitability low. The system was also subject to limited accountability. By the beginning of the 1990s, it was becoming evident that the system could not be sustained without a thorough revamping of its operations.

The BoP crisis in 1990–91 provided the trigger point for reform in several sectors, including the financial sector. The reform initiatives started with the government appointing two committees: one on BoP under the chairmanship of Dr C. Rangarajan, which went into the liberalization of policies in the external sector; and the second, on the financial sector under the chairmanship of M. Narasimham, which deliberated on domestic financial sector reforms. The reform programme in the financial sector, after 1992, largely followed the broad approach set out by these two committees, supplemented by the second Narasimham Committee, which was set up in 1997.

With regard to the 'arithmeticals' of reform in the financial sector—to use a term used by the Narasimham Committee—significant progress was made in the 1990s. There was a steady decline in the level of resource pre-emption from the banking system. Both the CRR and the SLR were reduced from their high levels—15 per cent and 38.5 per cent respectively in 1991–92—to 9 per cent and 25 per cent respectively. Interest rates in various segments of financial markets were deregulated in a phased manner. This preceded the abolition of controls on capital issues and freeing of interest rate on private bonds and debentures. While the government borrowing rates were market-determined, there was a gradual phasing out of interest rate subsidies on bank loans. Wide-ranging reforms were initiated to develop and deepen the government securities market, money market, capital market and foreign exchange market. The so-called Bank Rate was reactivated, regular short-term Repos at a pre-announced rate were being conducted and a system of prime lending rate was introduced to provide direction to the movement of interest rates in the credit market.

In the sphere of external financial policy, while the exchange rate was market-determined, over the years, there was a progressive liberalization of foreign direct and portfolio investment, and approval procedures were considerably simplified. As a result, restrictions on the inflow of capital into the economy were significantly reduced. There was also a significant liberalization of policy regarding the industry's access to foreign equity and borrowing through long-term debt instruments. The banking sector was given a greater degree of freedom with regard to raising funds abroad and managing their external liability, subject to prudential guidelines. The end result of all these and other reforms was the growing integration among various segments of financial markets, closer convergence of the Indian financial system with practices prevailing in international financial markets, and greater opportunity for investors to access both domestic and international markets.

Competitive conditions in the banking industry were facilitated by relaxing the entry and exit norms and permitting public sector banks to raise additional capital from the market (up to a certain level). While public sector banks continued to be predominant, the changing competitive environment in the banking sector made a substantial difference in banking practices and disclosure requirements.

Prudential regulation and supervision also formed a critical component of the financial sector reform programme. India adopted international prudential norms and practices with regard to capital adequacy, income recognition, provisioning requirement and supervision. These norms were progressively tightened over the years, particularly against the backdrop of the East Asian crisis. The required capital adequacy ratio was increased to 9 per cent, from 8 per cent, in the banking sector. The mark-to-market practice for valuation of government securities was also gradually enhanced from 30 per cent in 1992–93 to 75 per cent by 1999–2000. As a further prudential measure against credit and market risks, risk weights were made applicable to government and other securities to take account of price variations.

An attempt was also made to avoid the problems arising from 'connected lending'. The exposure of individual banks and NBFCs to any particular borrower or groups of borrowers was prescribed and the banking system's exposure to real estate was also limited. Prudent limits were placed on the financial system and the corporate sector, regarding foreign borrowings.

In the area of supervision, a full-fledged institutional mechanism was developed keeping in view the needs of a strong and stable financial system. The system of off-site surveillance was combined with periodical on-site supervision for monitoring the risk profile of banks and their compliance with prudential guidelines. The Basel Committee on Banking Supervision's Core Principles for Effective Banking Supervision were adopted, and the rating system for Indian banks was also introduced. The RBI's regulatory and supervisory responsibility was widened to include financial institutions and non-banking financial companies.

As a result of these and other measures, some progress in the performance of the Indian banking system was noticeable. The trend in the erosion of profit and capital base was reversed. The net profits of the public sector banks, as a percentage of their total assets, averaged 0.4 per cent during 1994–95 to 1998–99, against the loss of about 1 per cent in 1992–93 and 1993–94. The gross NPAs of public sector banks (without allowing for provisions), as a percentage of total assets, declined. Most of the public sector banks achieved the prescribed capital adequacy ratios. The improved performance also enabled most of the banks to meet their capital requirements from internal resources and the market, without excessive dependence on budgetary support.

The consolidation of the financial system during the second half of the 1990s increased the resilience of the Indian economy towards external crisis. This was evident from the muted impact of the Asian crisis on the Indian financial markets. Since then, there has been a constant effort to enhance the regulatory and supervisory standards in conformity with international standards.

The Way Ahead

There has been a widespread interest and debate among experts and market participants globally on the various aspects of financial reform which enabled India to chart out the path best suited for it. Looking ahead, a few areas which deserve attention in the context of recent developments in the global economy are mentioned below.

In recent years, there has been an explosive growth in the size and depth of financial markets, and in their globalization. In the context of fast-growing global financial assets, private financial flows to emerging markets have skyrocketed. By now, they far surpass official capital flows that had been the main source of foreign capital to developing economies since the end of World War II. Simultaneously, domestic financial markets in fast-growing emerging markets, including India, expanded rapidly. These developments have helped raise domestic savings and investment rates. Equally importantly, they have led to improvements in the capital allocation process by enhanced market discipline. The combined result (together with better policies) has been a higher economic growth.

While this globalization of financial markets and explosion in private capital flows has been mostly positive, it has to be recognized that these have also substantially increased the risks from external factors. In the light of the repeated financial crises during the past three decades, developing economies need to realize that there is an urgent need to examine the role of finance from a new, complex, interactive and systemic perspective. Risks from geopolitical threats, demographics, technology and climate change may be huge. To offset these risks, countries should give much greater weight to the markets, to rebalance the current overdependence on debt. This will increase system resilience and promote risk-sharing, thus enhancing the resilience of the entire financial system and reducing possibilities of future financial crises.

In this context, an important priority for the future is to continue with the process of strengthening India's prudential, provisioning and capitalization norms and bringing them in line with the best international standards. It is equally important to continue with efforts to introduce maximum transparency, disclosure and accountability so that investors and counter parties to financial transactions can take their decisions based on full information and their own assessment of market and other risks. Tighter and tougher prudential standards will no doubt cause some pain and impose greater responsibility on banks and other financial institutions. However, given the new international focus and externalities and linkages involved, the regulation of the financial sector is no longer a matter of choice or domestic concern alone. Over a period of time, it is likely that the willingness of the rest of the world to do financial business—either by way of trade credits, direct investments or other types of investments and loans—will depend on their confidence in India's financial practices. India must, thus, remain ahead of the curve in its prudential management.

The level of NPAs of the banking system in India has shown substantial increase in the past few years. Currently, part of the problem in resolving this issue is the carry-over of old NPAs in certain declining sectors of the industry. The problem has been further complicated by the fact that there are a few banks which are fundamentally weak and their potential to return to profitability, without substantial restructuring, is doubtful. Leaving aside the problem of weak banks, in profitable banks also, the NPA levels were relatively high. Recently, in 2017, the government initiated some significant measures to enforce the Insolvency and Bankruptcy Code (IBC), 2016, and introduced measures to hold large corporate borrowers accountable to repay their outstanding debts to banks as early as feasible.

The ordinance issued by the government also empowered the RBI to 'issue directions to any banking company to initiate insolvency resolution process in respect of a default under the provisions of the Insolvency and Bankruptcy Code'. The amended law also empowered the central bank to set up 'oversight panels' to shield bankers from later action by regulatory agencies looking into loan recasts—a recalculation of the loan value and the payments required—which was one of the purported reasons that banks had hesitated, thus far, to take firm action against defaulters.

On 12 June 2017, the RBI took another step in its bid to resolve the crisis. Its internal advisory committee identified twelve corporate accounts that each owed at least ₹5,000 crore, of which three-fifths had been classified as non-performing as of 31 March 2016. The RBI then recommended that these loans be recovered via insolvency proceedings under the newly enacted IBC, which has prescribed a deadline for the resolution of outstanding credits given by banks. The resolution has to be done before the deadline. Otherwise, the company's assets have to be liquidated to repay the loan. Experts say that India's new insolvency and bankruptcy law has been inspired by a similar law in the UK, which has been in place for thirty years.

In future, a vigorous effort has to be made by all banks to strengthen their internal control and risk-management systems, and to set up early-warning signals for timely detection and action. Henceforth, the resolution of the NPA problem also requires greater accountability on the part of corporates, timely disclosures in the case of defaults and an efficient credit information system. With the help of stricter accounting and prudential standards, the problem of NPAs could be effectively contained in the future.

Over the years, the progressive liberalization of financial markets and institutional reforms has led to growing inter-linkages among various segments of financial markets. The emergence of different types of financial intermediaries, in addition to banks and financial institutions, is healthy and desirable. A diversified structure contributes to greater stability of the financial system in the event of unanticipated problems. Part of the reason why problems in the financial sector in several fast-growing countries have persisted for so long is believed to be due to virtually 'bank-only' financial intermediation. In India, while there has been progress in developing various segments of markets, including money and debt markets, the depth of these markets remains shallow and the volume as well as number of participants are not very large. An important priority for the future is to develop the depth and breadth of these markets and to allow multiplicity of intermediation possibilities, with different risks and leverage profiles.

Apart from the banks, India has a number of NBFCs. The fundamental difference between banks and NBFCs in India is that the latter do not form part of the payment and settlement system, and the deposit insurance facility is also not available to depositors of NBFCs, unlike in the case of banks. The NBFCs are far from being homogenous, and include many diverse types of financial institutions: from a housing finance company to an equipment leasing company. The diversity among the entities of the NBFC sector is also reflected in attributes like the sizes and extent of regulatory oversight. In 2017, there were nearly 12,000 NBFCs registered with the RBI, of which a little over 200 NBFCs were deposit-accepting with an asset size of ₹1 billion or more.

Traditionally, the regulation of NBFCs was confined to deposit-taking activities. In 1997, the RBI was given comprehensive powers to regulate them. The amended RBI Act made it mandatory for every NBFC to have minimum net-owned funds and obtain a certificate of registration from the RBI for commencing or carrying on business. At the current juncture, while a large chunk of deposit- and non-deposit-taking financial companies are regulated by the RBI, housing finance companies are regulated by the National Housing Bank, chit funds are regulated by the state governments, and mutual benefit companies are regulated by the Ministry of Corporate Affairs. This multiplicity of regulators has always become an issue in their functioning.

In future, a sensitive and controversial question which would also need to be faced, sooner or later, is whether the 'public sector character' of our banks and other institutions which dominate

India's banking sector, is consistent with their being able to play a globally competitive role. In order to consider this issue dispassionately, both the advantages and disadvantages associated with this particular characteristic of the financial system have to be recognized.

An important advantage is the reduced 'vulnerability' of the system as a whole, because of sovereign ownership. Another important advantage is its wide reach and the availability of an established institutional infrastructure. Important disadvantages, however, are the relative insensitivity of the system to its cost structure, inability to respond quickly to the changing market trends and greater rigidities in the management decision-making processes because of what may be described as 'non-commercial' considerations. The development of human resources and introduction of an appropriate incentive structure to foster a competitive culture have, in this context, proved to be particularly difficult.

Can some of these intrinsic disadvantages of public sector institutions be overcome? The answer to this question is not very clear. It is true that almost all the leading banks and financial institutions in the world today are in the private sector. At the same time, it is equally true that the private sector character of a country's banking system has been no guarantee of its global success or its economic strength. As is well known, in 2007–08, even in the US, which had the largest financial sector in the global economy, there was a deep financial crisis which took several years to resolve.

In India, with necessary will and a political consensus, in principle it should be possible to grant complete functional and operational independence to public sector banks and institutions, by legislation. Their primary objective should be to provide the best service at the least cost and, thus, enable them to compete freely among themselves as well as with other private sector institutions. If, in practice, this is not a feasible option, then the only alternative is for public sector banks to be transformed into widely held private banking corporations, subject to transparency, regulations and accountability to shareholders.

The long-term vision for India's banking system to transform itself from being largely a domestic one to a global one may sound far-fetched. However, it is not beyond our capacity, provided we have the will and the determination. Taking the entire banking industry to the heights of international excellence by 2025 will require a combination of new technologies, better processes of credit and risk appraisal, treasury management, product diversification, internal control and external regulations and, not the least, human resources. Fortunately, we have a comparative advantage in almost all these areas. Our professionals are at the forefront of technological change and financial developments all over the world. It is time to harness these resources for development of the Indian banking sector so that India becomes a major international financial centre by 2025.

There are some specific characteristics of money and finance which make it particularly amenable for India's domestic banking sector to realize the full benefits from Information Technology (IT):

- Unlike most other goods and services, and in respect of money and finance, no physical movement or physical delivery is required to complete transactions and their end use. As a result, in recent years, financial volumes, with the aid of electronics and computerization, have grown phenomenally. As such, the total financial transactions in

- a day can exceed the entire GDP of a country.
- In the financial sector, credits and debits need to be settled in real time so that value risk and default risk are minimized. Earlier, when the payment and settlement system was based on the movement of papers, it took several days to reconcile debits and credits. Today, payment and settlements can happen on a real-time basis.
- A related characteristic is that, with the possibility of payment and settlement taking place simultaneously in real time, risks and uncertainties can be reduced. This reduces the cost of capital, and has tremendous advantages for increasing productivity and generating higher output at lower cost. It has also made it possible to devise complex financial products, such as derivatives, without adding to the risk or uncertainty, which has expanded the scope for meeting various kinds of financial preferences, risk profiles and requirements of savers and investors.

In India, these characteristics represent a tremendous plus for the growth of IT in finance. There are, however, certain limitations regarding financial transactions vis-à-vis e-commerce of physical products. There is a greater need for a supervisory and regulatory system, since many financial institutions such as banks, mutual funds, pension funds, etc. deal with other people's money. It is important to ensure that people's savings are safe and not diverted or misused.

The financial system can also be highly leveraged. In order to safeguard investors' interests, it becomes necessary to impose some limits on leveraging in relation to the size of the owned funds. A related requirement is that the total volume of money in the system has to be related to the size of the real economy. In other words, financial agencies, unless specifically authorized to do so, cannot be allowed to create 'new' money. Otherwise, money itself will lose its value and the economy could be characterized by high inflation.

Over time, the increasing use of IT in finance is inevitable, and we are going to see a very large percentage of transactions taking place through the Internet and World Wide Web even in semi-urban areas. At the same time, much greater supervision, surveillance and regulation of monetary transactions conducted electronically or over the Internet, are going to be required. These systems are yet to fully evolve, particularly in smaller cities. India has already set up the Indian Financial Network (an electronic real-time gross settlement system) and faster computerization of bank branches. Recently, the government also announced its intention to set up a computer emergency response team for the financial sector to provide domain expertise and coordination in this sector.

Another important issue in respect of the long-term stability of the financial sector, which has been extensively discussed in the literature, as well as on different international forums, is that of an appropriate exchange rate regime, particularly for emerging markets. It is now well-established that the appropriate management of the financial sector has to be compatible with the so-called impossible trinity—namely, full capital account convertibility, monetary independence (for inflation control) and a stable currency.

If capital account convertibility is accepted, according to accepted theory, a country either has the choice of giving up monetary independence and setting up a currency board or has to give up the stable currency objective. Exchange rate has to float freely so that monetary policy can then be directed to the objectives of inflation control. In this scenario, the exchange rate should matter only if it affects domestic inflation. In theory, the recommended approach is either free float or a currency board.

In reality, however, the actual policy adopted by most central banks is different than the theoretical optimum. By far, the most common exchange rate regime adopted by countries, including industrial countries, is neither a currency board nor a free float. Most of the countries have adopted intermediate regimes of various types, including fixed pegs, crawling pegs, fixed rates within bands, managed floats with no pre-announced path and independent floats with foreign exchange intervention moderating the rate of change and preventing undue fluctuations. By and large, countries have 'managed' floats, or central banks intervene periodically. Traditionally, this is also true of the European Union and Japan. The US also recently intervened in favour of moderating the movements of its currency. It is, thus, a matter of fact that, irrespective of the pure theoretical position of a currency board or a free float, the external value of the currency continues to be a matter of concern to most countries and most central banks.

Part of the reason why countries are concerned about exchange rates is psychological, and part is real. It is psychological because of the headline effect of a depreciating currency—'all time low', 'weak', 'tumbling'—which creates a false impression about, and has a negative impact on, the soundness of a country's currency. The contagion effect of sharp movements in exchange is also quick and it can affect the real economy. Exporters may suffer if there is unanticipated and sharp appreciation, and debtors or other corporates may be affected badly if there is a sharp depreciation, which can also lead to bank failures and bankruptcies.

A fundamental change that has taken place in recent years is the importance of capital flows in determining exchange rate movements as against trade deficits and economic growth, which were important in the earlier period. The latter do matter, but only over a period of time. Capital flows, on the one hand, are primary determinants of exchange rate movements on a day-to-day basis. Capital flows in 'gross' terms, which affect the exchange rate, can also be several times higher than 'net' flows on any day—and these are also much more sensitive to what everybody else is saying or doing, than is the case with foreign trade or economic growth. Therefore, herding becomes unavoidable. All dealers prefer to be wrong with everyone else rather than being wrong alone! In this situation, as past experience shows, the central banks have to intervene in some form or other—including the mightiest and the not so mighty. While the degree of intervention and management varies from central bank to central bank, concerns about exchange rates is a fact that every country has to face.

A related issue that has figured in the literature is that if some management of the exchange rate is required, what is it that a country should be monitoring—nominal effective exchange rate or real effective exchange rate? From a competitive point of view, and also from the medium-term perspective, it is the latter which should be monitored as it reflects changes in the external value of a currency in relation to its trading partners in real terms. However, it is not effective for monitoring short-term and day-to-day movements, as 'nominal' rates are the ones which are most sensitive of capital flows and also attract the most headlines. Over the long term, it is also important for India to keep a close and constant vigilance over movements in exchange rates in international currencies, particularly the dollar and euro. India's exchange rate policy should also be fully compatible with its BoP requirements and financing trade deficits. In case higher capital inflows are needed, the RBI, in consultation with the government, should be prepared to change its current exchange rate policy over time to respond to the emerging situation.

By and large, recent changes in the global financial sector have brought tremendous benefits to the developing world, including India. Capital and technological constraints on development are fast disappearing. As new horizons open up, we are also faced with some new challenges. With an appropriate policy response, India and some other countries will be able to take maximum advantage of technological and other advances, while minimizing risks.

The above are just a few priority areas which can be effectively implemented over the next few years and will certainly improve the functioning of India's economy. These suggestions are, by no means, exhaustive. If India gets them right, it would speed up the movement in other areas of financial reforms and contribute to making India one of the fastest-growing developing countries.

7

The Role of Government and Administrative Reforms

The reasons for India opting for a highly controlled State-dominated development strategy after Independence in 1947 are well known. The economic profile of the country at that time was distressing. There was hardly any growth in the previous half-century, and both agriculture and industry were characterized by severe structural distortions. Like other underdeveloped countries, India was an exporter of cheap primary products and an importer of industrial products, with a secular decline in its terms of trade and stagnation in its per capita incomes. During the first half of this century, the rate of growth of national income was less than 1 per cent per year, which was comparable to the rate of population growth during this period. In real terms, therefore, at the time of Independence, the average Indian was as badly off as he or she had been at the turn of the century. Against this background, there was unanimity among nationalist intellectuals, political leaders and industrialists about the preferred directions of economic strategy after Independence. The need for the government to occupy commanding heights and to lead from the top, received further support from the astounding success of the erstwhile Soviet Union in emerging as a rival centre to the West, with respect to political and industrial power, within a very short period. India, at that time, played a pioneering role in giving expression to the aspirations of the newly independent developing countries in the economic field. Following the example of the Soviet Union, there was also a broad consensus on many of the strategic issues, such as the vital role of the public sector, discouragement of foreign investment, development of heavy industries and need for centralized allocation of resources.

The expansion of the government's role in practically all spheres of the economy in the last fifty years occurred gradually and haphazardly in response to new problems and political compulsion. Each step had a logic of its own and consideration was not given to their cumulative impact on the economy. Thus, in the 1950s, since savings and incomes were low, it seemed natural for the government to take on the task of mobilizing incremental savings through taxation and market borrowings. The base of entrepreneurship, as in many other developing countries, was small and concentrated in some regions of the country. Large investments required in the steel and machine-building sectors could only be undertaken directly by the government in view of the underdeveloped financial sector. By the end of the 1960s, the concentration of economic power in a few business houses became a major political and economic issue; this further strengthened the role of the State in the industrial sphere. Banks were nationalized in order to break the nexus between the private industry and finance, and to make credit available to traditionally underfunded sectors, such as agriculture and the small scale industry.

While the reasons for adopting a centrally directed strategy of development were understandable against the background of colonial rule, it soon became clear that the actual results of this strategy were far below expectations. Instead of showing a high growth, high public savings and high degree of self-reliance, India was actually showing one of the lowest rates of growth in the developing world, with rising public deficits and periodic BoP crises. According to one calculation, in the thirty out of forty years between 1950 and 1990, India had BoP problems of varying intensities. Looking back, it is hard to believe that for as long as four decades after 1950, India's growth rates averaged less than 4 per cent per annum and the per capita income growth was less than 2 per cent per annum. This was at a time when the developing world, including Sub-Saharan Africa, and other least developed countries, showed a growth rate of 5.2 per cent per annum.

However, the most striking failure was not in terms of growth, or even in the precarious situation of the BoP. Although the argument is not convincing, it could still be claimed that the low growth outcome was on account of a number of factors beyond India's control, such as the border wars, severe droughts, periodic oil shocks, and, finally, the inhospitable global environment. The BoP difficulties could also be attributed to the global woes of primary producers and the struggle of a poor developing country like India to industrialize and become self-reliant in the heavy industry sector (which previously had been the monopoly of the rich industrialized countries). The most conspicuous failure, for which there is no justifiable reason, is the erosion in public savings and the inability of the public sector to generate resources for investment or the provision of public services.

Performance of the Public Sector

It will be recalled that an important assumption in the choice of a post-Independence development strategy was the generation of public savings, which could be used for higher levels of investment. However, this did not happen and the public sector, instead of being a generator of savings for the community's good, became a consumer of the community's savings. This reversal in roles had become evident by the early 1970s and the process reached its culmination by the early 1980s. By then the government had begun to borrow not only to meet its own revenue expenditure, but also to finance public sector deficits and investments. In the period between 1960 to 1975, the total public sector borrowings (including government borrowings) averaged 4.4 per cent of GDP. These increased to 6 per cent of GDP by 1980–81, and further to 9 per cent by 1989–90.

Thus, the public sector, which had a commanding presence in almost all industrial sectors of the economy, particularly the heavy industry, gradually became a net drain on the society as a whole. It is interesting to note that the central government's total internal public debt reached a stupendous ₹5,00,000 crore by mid-1990, and nearly one-third of it was accounted for by assets held in the public sector. Interest payments on public debt, at that time, amounted to nearly ₹40,000 crore, which were financed by new net borrowings and represented nearly 70 per cent of the centre's fiscal deficit. In effect, one-third of the interest payments were on account of the government's past investment in the public sector. By the end of the 1990s, the Centre's internal debt almost doubled to ₹9,70,000 crore. Since then, by 2017, there had been a six-fold increase in India's public debt and its level had reached ₹60,66,000 crore. This amounted to nearly

70 per cent of India's total GDP. The sharp increase in public debt, over time, partly accounts for the need to borrow higher amounts each year to service past debt, rather than increase the rate of growth in public investment.

Looking back at the performance of the public sector in contributing to national savings (which has been negative for the past five decades), it is amazing how much of the economic and political debate on future strategy is still conditioned by the pre-1947 colonial experience and special interests. Irrespective of which party or coalition of parties is in power, political leaders (with very few exceptions) express their confidence in the ability of the public sector to generate savings. Disinvestment targets, particularly for loss-making units, may be announced from time to time, but are unlikely to be reached. Ministries in charge of loss-making public sector units also regularly announce their intentions to revive these units by making further investments, even though they are fully aware of the dismal results of such efforts.

The primary issue here is not public sector versus private sector or the ideological predilections in favour of a state-dominated development strategy vis-à-vis a market-dominated strategy. Nor is it about the virtues of globalization or its discontents. The issue is simply about the proper use of national savings in an environment of rising revenue deficits. Is it appropriate to use these savings for financing further losses of the public sector units which are of no particular interest or service to the vast majority of India's poor? Is it appropriate to continue with large government borrowings and the disproportionate burden of interest payments on the government's budget when earlier borrowings invested in the public sector had not given adequate returns? There is no doubt that the financial interests of workers in the public sector, whether these units are yielding returns or not, deserve to be protected. The crucial issue is whether the most economically efficient way of protecting these interests is through further government borrowings to finance mounting losses and low returns in these units; or, whether these interests can be adequately protected through a more productive use of the capital (including land) that is locked up in these units.

The Administrative System

The hangover of the past is also reflected in the continuing dominant role of the bureaucracy in determining policy outcomes. A basic premise of India's Plans as well as the early development literature, was that the required administrative response to fulfil the ambitious public investment targets and regulate the economy, would be forthcoming in ample measure at different levels of administration—from the Centre to the village level. The administration was expected to work in complete harmony to selflessly carry out the various tasks in public interest. While most of the economy was still in private hands, a large bureaucracy was nurtured to regulate and control it. Thus, under India's early Plans, 'a burgeoning bureaucracy became the surrogate for socialism'.[11] By the early 1960s, when the Third Plan was launched, it had become clear that the expansion of administrative responsibilities was itself an important cause of inefficiency and delay. The Third Plan document was frank enough to observe that 'as large burdens are thrown on the administrative structure, it grows in size and as its size increases, it becomes slower in its functioning. Delays

---

[11]Basu, K. (Ed.). (2004). *India's emerging economy: Performance and prospects in the 1990s and beyond.* MIT press.

occur and affect operations at every stage and the expected outputs are further deferred'.[12]

Although the problem was recognized more than five decades ago, the proliferation of the bureaucracy has continued unabated and the administrative structure has become less and less functional despite significant liberalization of the economy after 1991. On all counts, the old bureaucratic and regulatory framework has become even more cumbersome. More and more agencies have been set up to regulate, control or oversee agencies set up earlier. A business environment survey carried out by the World Bank revealed that managers reported spending 5 per cent of their time dealing with government officials in Latin American countries, and about twice that, in the transition economies of Eastern Europe. In India, the average share of the time that managers spent in dealing with bureaucracy, even after the economic reforms of the 1990s, was more than 15 per cent.

In addition to the regulatory control and several inspections imposed by federal agencies, there is a plethora of administrative rules and regulations imposed by state and local governments. These differ from state to state, and from district to district within a state. Small and medium firms are the worst affected as they tend to have less developed political contacts for overcoming administrative barriers.

Priorities for the Future

It's important to understand the priority areas where further long-term reforms and policy initiatives are required to achieve India's full potential as an emerging global power by 2025.

---

[12]'The Third Five Year Plan', Government of India, 1961.

The Role of Government and Administrative Reforms

An important priority for the future is to redefine the primary role of the government in the economy. This is a difficult issue as the government is directly responsible for initiating political and economic reforms for the people in order to alleviate poverty and accelerate India's growth as a global emerging power. Nevertheless, as it happens, despite some important measures to liberalize domestic and international control in respect of production, trade and capital flows, India still remains one of the most heavily regulated economies in the world. In fact, over time, despite liberalization, the role of the government (including state governments) has expanded practically in all spheres of the economy.

Over time, the number of ministries and departments involved in regulating almost all segments of the economy, society, foreign affairs, defence and border security have expanded enormously. In addition to the traditional ministries, such as Finance, Defence, Home, Commerce and Industry, etc., we now also have ministries such as Micro, Small and Medium Enterprises; Labour and Employment; Skill Development and Entrepreneurship; AYUSH (**A**yurveda, **Y**oga and Naturopathy, **U**nani, **S**iddha and **H**omoeopathy); Culture; Tourism; Social Justice and Empowerment; Youth Affairs and Sports; and so on. The number of Cabinet ministers and ministers of state in 2017 is as high as seventy-five. All the announced policies that different ministries handle, in association with other concerned ministries with similar roles, naturally take a long time to be implemented on the ground, particularly in rural and underdeveloped areas of the country.

In 2019 and beyond, an important challenge will be to redefine the role of the government, irrespective of which party or combination of parties are in power. At the macroeconomic level, the political (i.e. ministerial) role of the government should be to ensure a stable and competitive environment with a strong external sector and a transparent domestic administrative system. While the macroeconomic priorities (for example, the so-called trade-off between growth and inflation) may be decided by the government, the instrumentalities for achieving these objectives must be left to autonomous regulatory and promotional agencies. Similarly, the government's direct role in economic areas should be reset in favour of ensuring the availability of public goods (such as roads and water) and essential services (such as health and education) to the people. In these areas, the government's role must expand substantially. At the same time, its role in managing commercial enterprises deserves to be correspondingly reduced.

A related area, both at the Centre and states, is transparency in the decision-making process within the government. A major step in this respect has been taken with the enactment of the RTI. The beneficial impact of this legislation in making the government accountable and citizen-friendly is already visible. A further step in this direction should be to make it mandatory for all ministries and departments of the government to voluntarily make information, on the decisions taken by them, available to the public (excluding security-related subjects). It may be clarified that information should be released by the ministries themselves, without the need for any member of the public to ask for it. If this is done, the free media and civil society institutions will constitute an effective instrument for enforcing accountability in the decision-making process itself.

Another administrative priority is to reduce the discretionary power of ministers in allocation of public resources. Why should a minister decide who should be allotted the telecom spectrum, or the mining rights for iron ore or copper, or the merger of public sector enterprises? Let the concerned minister and Cabinet collectively decide only on the policy for allocations. However, the question of which entity should be given allocations, should be left entirely to an autonomous agency with adequate powers.

India has some highly distinguished public institutions, such as the EC, Central Information Commission and UPSC, which have rendered excellent service to the country. Appointments to these institutions are made by the government. However, once appointed, members have full authority to carry out the tasks assigned to them without any interference or approval by the concerned ministries. Similar autonomous institutions should be created for the allocation of all valuable national resources, including oil and gas.

Except in selected areas, such as security and defence, it is desirable to cut through elaborate red tape, and implement, as soon as feasible, the policy of permitting 'self-certification' by Chief Executives of registered companies and organizations. Such simplification, which automatically reduces the demand and supply of corruption, has already been introduced in some areas with perceptible success (for example, foreign exchange regulations). There is simply no reason why India cannot have a rule-based system of administration, which is not dependent on ministerial discretion on a case-to-case basis.

It is also necessary to further simplify administrative procedures and reduce the number of agencies, at different levels, involved in providing clearances for undertaking any activity. For example, at least thirty different clearances involving several agencies at the Centre and the states are required for setting up even a modest-sized industrial factory. Except in selected areas where strict timelines can be prescribed for giving approvals (such as, forest and environment clearances), it is desirable to cut through the elaborate red tape and rely primarily on self-certification. The government can lay down standards and norms (for example, in respect of pollution or fire safety) and the entity concerned may be required to 'self-certify' at the highest levels of management that these have been complied with as per the notified procedures. Government agencies can make random checks and in case there are clear-cut violations, appropriate penal action can be taken. Similarly, the present complexity in regulations should be reduced drastically.

In order to simplify the administrative procedure, it is also essential to reduce the large number of persons who are hired as civil servants, across a large number of ministries, at different levels and in several departments, to design, coordinate and implement similar policies. At present, there is a built-in reluctance to simplify administrative procedures as, over time, this may lead to a large number of staff members with nothing much to do in their existing offices. To overcome this problem, while simplifying procedures, the government should also announce that all the administrative staff currently employed, will remain in office until their retirement, with full pensions. In order to facilitate this process, the government can also introduce an 'early retirement scheme' which would permit members of staff who do not have sufficient office work, to retire if they wish to do so earlier than their pre-scheduled retirement date.

A further measure for the greater empowerment of civil service personnel, while reducing their number over time, is to reform the procedure for launching vigilance inquiries and the number of agencies involved in such investigations. The ease with which investigations can be launched without adequate cause, and then closed after several years for lack of evidence, is a major cause of harassment and pain for honest civil servants at higher levels. Civil servants often avoid taking a decision according to the rules in place, on a financial or controversial matter, without seeking ministerial approval. In case a decision on such a matter is taken by a civil servant (who is authorized to do so), it is feared that an inquiry may be launched at the insistence of a minister or a business group, who/that will be adversely affected by that decision. The fear of taking decisions is a major cause of delays and atrophy in the decision-making process.

The basic issue that needs to be tackled to improve the morale of civil servants is that of the 'separation of powers' within the executive—between ministers and civil servants—in so far as posting, transfers, promotions and other similar administrative matters are concerned. The separation of powers among the three branches of the government—the executive, the legislature and the judiciary—is already enshrined in the Constitution. Although there has been considerable encroachment by the executive into legislative and even judicial areas, it can still be said that these three separate branches enjoy a substantial measure of autonomy and independence (if they wish to exercise it). Within the executive branch, however, the civil service is now completely dependent on the pleasure of the ministers in regard to even the most mundane and routine administrative matters. It is essential to revert to a rule-based system of administration, which circumscribes the powers of politicians and confers greater authority on the civil service itself, for self-regulation.

The greater empowerment of the civil service must, of course, go hand in hand with a greater accountability on the part of civil servants for their performance and conduct. While within the executive branch, the civil service has lost power, as far as the public is concerned, it is still the most powerful agency of the State. By all accounts, for various reasons, India has now acquired the unenviable distinction of having one of the most elaborate multi-level administrative systems, particularly in its dealings with the average citizen. As highlighted earlier, bureaucratic corruption (in addition to political corruption) is also the root cause of lower productivity in the use of resources and the fiscal disempowerment of the State.

By 2025, the relative roles of the Central and state governments in the economy should also be redefined. The Central government must withdraw altogether from the implementation, monitoring or direction of economic programmes in all spheres. The main role of the Centre should be the management of a macroeconomic policy, and the definition and enforcement of the legal framework for economic activities, including the movement of goods, services and people across state boundaries. The implementation of economic programmes should be the responsibility of state governments. The devolution of central revenues and distribution of Plan grants/loans should continue to be governed, like it is presently done by periodic Finance Commission reports. The system of financial transfers between the Centre and the states, despite some drawbacks, has worked reasonably well over the years without being overly contentious.

At the same time, from an economic point of view, there is also enough evidence to suggest that overcentralization is an important cause of inefficiency and the diversion of resources from production to administration. Past experience does not show that centralized planning for allocation of budgetary expenditure for investments leads to more efficient planning or implementation. Politically, with the emergence of strong regional parties, and with several different parties in power at the Centre and in the states, the decentralization of economic power is essential. Recently, the Central government has taken measures to transfer some administrative powers for the implementation of certain programmes announced by it, particularly for transfer of subsidies to the poor.

Among the important reforms introduced by the government, perhaps the most significant measure, which was pending for several years, is the implementation of the GST Act in 2017. However, as finally approved by a consensus among the Centre and states, the structure of the GST Act is highly complex. There is not one uniform GST across different goods and services, but as many as five rates: 0 per cent, 5 per cent, 12 per cent, 18 per cent and 28 per cent. There are also some goods and services that are not covered under the announced rates. In a few cases, local bodies, such as municipal corporations, can also impose their own taxes. In view of the complexity of the present GST structure and its implementation across diverse states in due course, an important priority for the future is to move to one reasonable and relatively low GST rate to cover all taxable goods and services across the country. This reform in the GST structure may take some time to be implemented, based on the actual experience on the ground in different states, particularly as regards to the supply and demand of essential goods and services under the present Act.

State governments now have the major responsibility for the implementation of economic and social programmes for the improvement of their cities and villages, and for the betterment of their people. The need for a vigorous programme to improve the physical infrastructure and to expand the reach of primary education and basic healthcare is now urgent. If governments do more of what they alone can do (e.g. access to primary education or health services for the poor) and less of what they cannot do effectively (e.g. operate commercial enterprises), the country would benefit greatly.

The above is a selective list of priorities which can be implemented over the next few years with political consensus among different parties at the Centre and states, with the approval of the Parliament and legislative assemblies across the country. India, today, has the capacity to achieve its full potential as an emerging global power, provided we have the necessary will and determination. The innate capacity of the people is immense and has been demonstrated beyond reasonable doubt. India's open and participative system of demonstration ensures that a change, where necessary, can be delayed, but it cannot be avoided altogether.

8

The Twenty-first Century is India's Century

During the fifty years after Independence, India's economic record was relatively poor. The total national income grew by about 4 per cent per annum. The per capita income, or income per head, grew by a meagre 1.9 per cent per annum on an average. As a result, despite high rates of growth in the twenty-first century, India's rank on various poverty indices remains low. According to World Bank's report, 30 per cent of Indians live below the so-called 'poverty line',[13] i.e. their income and consumption are even less than half of India's already low average per capita income.

India now has the opportunity and potential to achieve, in the first quarter of the twenty-first century, what it could not achieve in the previous fifty or hundred years: poverty elimination. Paradoxical as it may seem, in recent years, the patterns of global trade and investment have moved in India's favour and

---

[13]India has highest number of people living below poverty line: World Bank. (2016, October 03). Retrieved from https://www.businesstoday.in/current/economy-politics/india-has-highest-number-of-people-living-below-poverty-line-world-bank/story/238085.html

so has India's comparative advantage, which no longer lies in the production of low-value, low-technology, labour-intensive goods, but in relatively high-value, skill-intensive and high-technology products and services.

It is true that foreign trade and foreign investment have a relatively small share in India's national income and total investment. As such, a faster growth in these components alone cannot dramatically improve the outlook for poverty alleviation. However, a favourable shift could lead to a comparative advantage for India and make a crucial difference to the prospects for its BoP. Unlike the past, India's external trade and payments position are no longer constraints to growth, but are important sources of strength for the economy.

The sources of the comparative advantage of nations are vastly different today from what they were forty or fifty years ago. For example, forty years ago, developing countries were primarily producers of commodities (such as jute, rubber, tea and cotton) and the value added in manufacturing was largely captured by the industrial countries. This is no longer true. Developing countries have now emerged as major and competitive producers of manufactured products. Let us consider, for example, the following developments:

- Low- and middle-income countries now account for almost 80 per cent of the world's industrial workforce. What is even more striking is that, contrary to conventional thinking, developing countries' share of the world's skilled workforce also jumped from a third to nearly a half. Thus, industrialized countries no longer have a monopoly on manufacturing production, and developing countries are no longer exclusively dependent on the low-value trade of primary products.

The Twenty-first Century is India's Century

- A fast growth in manufacturing has been associated with a high rate of increase in employment and wages for workers across the developing world, including India.
- Growth has resulted in the movement of workers from low-wage agriculture and plantations to high-wage manufacturing jobs. In Malaysia, for example, in 1957, one in two employees worked on plantations. As a result of the high industrial growth since then, by 1990, only one in ten workers was engaged in plantation agriculture. Wage employment tripled between 1957 and 1990, while the share of the workforce employed in agriculture fell from 58 per cent to 26 per cent. This trend has continued in recent years also.
- Earlier, it was believed that the private sector did not have the resources to invest in a capital-intensive, large industry. In the past four decades, however, investment by the private sector in developing countries—in areas of infrastructure, and capital-intensive and long-gestation projects—has also increased substantially.

A number of factors account for why developing countries, in the present phase of the development of the world economy, have emerged as major producers and exporters of manufactured goods. First and foremost, the end of colonial rule and participation by developing countries in the post-war trade negotiations has significantly levelled international playing fields. Unlike the earlier periods of globalization in the late-nineteenth and early-twentieth centuries, the current trading pattern among different groups of countries, with some exceptions, reflects the real comparative advantage among nations. Interventionist strategies during the early years of the post-colonial period helped to establish an industrial base and an industrial culture in many developing countries, which could be used to exploit the new opportunities in international trade in the past four decades. This process was helped enormously by changes in the direction of foreign investment. Up to the end of World War II, foreign investment was entirely directed towards the production and trade of primary products (e.g., plantations, minerals and oil). In recent years, the bulk of foreign investment has gone into the manufacturing and service industries.

Another important factor which has helped the growth of developing countries' trade in manufacturing, is the cost-reducing technological changes of the last four decades. Technological change has made the accumulation of skills a more important factor in determining comparative advantage, than capital endowments. Developing countries which have benefited most from technological change are those where the level of skill formation and education have been high, as in countries in East Asia and China. Finally, the sharp decline in the costs of communication and transport has made geography, and proximity to markets, less relevant in influencing the choice of location for manufacturing.

The above changes have enabled developing countries to play a more decisive role in international trade. The extent to which different countries and regions have benefited from these trends has, of course, depended on country policies and their overall economic performance. Initial endowments and conditions (particularly in respect of education and health) have also played a role, but these, too, have been amenable to change.

Strengthening the Comparative Advantage

In view of the changes in India's economy in the last fifty years, as well as changes in the nature of foreign direct investment (FDI), there is a strong case now for treating all foreign equity investment in the same way as domestic corporate investment, subject to two, or possibly three, exceptions. One clear exception is defence and security-related industrial units (e.g., manufacture of armaments), where ownership and investment must be restricted, as far as feasible, to domestic corporations.

Secondly, there may be certain industries or activities which employ a large number of persons, but which have become uncompetitive because of technological changes or shifts in comparative advantage. If the entry of foreign companies in these traditional activities (or new substitutes) is likely to render a substantial number of persons unemployed, then there is a case for restricting foreign investment in these areas. Some agro-based activities, which employ millions of persons throughout the country, would deserve protection from foreign investment on this ground. However, it is important to ensure that such cases are considered exceptional and do not become generalized to cover uncompetitive and technologically outdated units in the modern industrial sector, where the employment angle is not very significant, as in electronic hardware. Over a period of time, as employment opportunities in the economy expand, workers may be expected to move out of low-productive jobs in the traditional sector to new industries and services.

A third exception, which is less clear-cut, is the discrimination against foreign investment on 'cultural' grounds. A case can be made to prevent the entry of, say, foreign films, or to restrict foreign investment in TV or radio stations in order to protect Indian culture and values. This, however, is a very slippery area. In a free and secular society, the determination of what are Indian values and what values deserve to be protected, cannot be left to bureaucrats or to a political party in power. An independent supervisory or regulatory body should perhaps be empowered to lay down standards and criteria which protect the country's interests and which have to be observed by domestic as well as foreign producers or investors.

As a result of conscious policy choices, until lately, India did not benefit greatly from the growth of the developing world's trade in manufacturing. In fact, India's share of world trade fell from about 2 per cent in 1950 to only 0.5 to 0.6 per cent in the 1990s. However, India, in the twenty-first century, is much better situated to take advantage of the sweeping technological changes than most other developing countries. It had the advantage of an early start in industrialization and in providing broad-based opportunities in skill-based education, including technological and managerial education. It can only be a matter of speculation regarding how much better off India would have been economically if it had seized its initial advantages to capture skills-related value addition in manufacturing.

The Services Revolution

In recent years, an even more phenomenal change from India's point of view is the growing role of skill-based services in determining the comparative advantage of economies. The development of certain services is now regarded as one of the preconditions of economic growth and not as one of its consequences. The boundary between goods and services is also disappearing, as services of various kinds are delinked from the manufacturing process and become essential elements of the productive structure.

The change in the role of services has been brought about by unprecedented and unforeseen advances in computer and communication technology over the last four decades. An important aspect of the 'services revolution' is that the geography and levels of industrialization are no longer the primary determinants of the location of facilities for the production of services. As a result, the traditional role of developing countries is also changing—from mere recipients to important providers of long-distance services. India, too, has participated in this changing scenario and exports of certain services (e.g. software) are expanding faster than the overall trade. The potential for expansion of jobs and incomes in the services sector is truly immense. From India's point of view, some of the global developments in recent years, which provide opportunities for substantial growth, are the following:

- The fastest-growing segment of services is knowledge-based services, such as professional and technical services, particularly in IT. India has a tremendous advantage in the supply of such services because of a developed structure of technological and educational institutions, and lower labour costs.
- Progress in IT is making it increasingly possible to unbundle the production and consumption of information-intensive service activities. These activities—inventory management, quality control, accounting, computing, personnel administration, and secretarial, marketing, advertising, distribution and legal services—are performed in all economic sectors. They play a fundamental role, not only in service industries but also in manufacturing and primary industries.
- Unlike most other prices, world prices of transport and communication services have fallen dramatically. The

most significant example in this area is provided by the Internet, which now links millions of computers around the world. Many large corporations are also building dedicated international networks to meet their global communication needs. India's geographical distance from several important industrial markets (for instance, North America) is no longer an important element in the cost structure of skill-based services.

- Technological innovation is expanding opportunities for services to be embodied in goods that are traded internationally. This means that India does not necessarily have to be a low-cost producer of certain types of goods (e.g. computers or discs) before it can become an efficient supplier of services embodied in them (e.g. software or music).

Fortunately, there are very few developing countries which are as well placed as India to take advantage of the phenomenal changes that have occurred in production technologies, international trade, capital movement and deployment of skilled manpower in the twenty-first century. A small but telling example of the change in our position over the last forty years is that, today, there are more Indian-origin managers in London, than British or American managers in Mumbai. India has acquired the knowledge and skills to build any project, manage any firm and contribute to the production and processing of a wide variety of industrial and consumer products.

If the recent growth performance of the Indian economy can be sustained at the level of 7 to 8 per cent per annum over the next ten years, extreme poverty in India can be virtually eliminated. The strong relationship that exists between sustained growth and reduction of poverty is an important conclusion that emerges from the recent economic history of developing countries. The higher the growth of the economy, the greater seems to be the capacity of the government to finance social expenditure. Higher government expenditure on the provision of social services, combined with a higher growth in employment opportunities (as a result of growth), can make a decisive impact on poverty levels.

It is no coincidence that countries and regions that have registered high and sustained rates of growth over a reasonable period of time are also the ones that have achieved the best results in reducing poverty and improving the health and nutrition-intake of their people. In some cases, progress in reducing poverty or improving the level of human development indicators has been much greater than would seem warranted by their rate of growth, as has happened in the Indian state of Kerala, as well as Sri Lanka. There are also cases where high growth has been combined with a worsening of the poverty ratio or where high per capita incomes have not resulted in adequate progress in education and other social services. However, such cases are not many and they have their own special reasons.

As we look ahead, over the long term, India has tremendous opportunities to alleviate poverty and to become one of the strongest global powers by 2025. As highlighted earlier, to achieve this goal and meet the challenges that lie ahead, we also need to initiate some political reforms which may take some time to implement after discussion and adoption of necessary legislative measures by the Parliament and state assemblies. We now have the ability to initiate reforms in the political and administrative system which can deliver public services to the people with least diversion, delay or multi-tier corruption in the allocation of public resources.

Epilogue
The India of Our Dreams

On 15 August 1947, when India became independent, in a celebrated and oft-quoted passage in his address to the nation, Jawaharlal Nehru said: 'Long years ago, we made a tryst with destiny and now the time comes when we shall redeem our pledge, not wholly or in full measure, but very substantially. At the stroke of the midnight hour, when the world sleeps, India will awake to life and freedom.' On the seventieth anniversary of our Independence, i.e. 15 August 2017, as we look back, there is certainly much to rejoice in what India has been able to achieve in the past seventy years. In view of India's poverty and diversity at the time of our Independence in 1947, not many political observers believed that the Indian democracy would survive for long. It is gratifying to note that our democratic system has not only survived, but is universally regarded as a role model for a peaceful transfer of power from one government to another after periodic elections.

Today, India is one of the few developing countries in the world, where so many people—a lot of them poor—cast their votes regularly in free and fair elections to choose their representatives.

The India of Our Dreams

The birth of India's democracy, after Independence, was also unique. Unlike many other established democracies of the time, India's democracy came into being, peacefully, and without a revolution or uprising by the people. It was put in place by its nationalist leaders; what was particularly remarkable was that all citizens were given the right to vote, irrespective of gender, caste, creed, religion, income, occupation or level of literacy.

The Indian economy, which for quite some time—in the 1950s, 60s and 70s—was in doldrums, has also recovered and shown rapid and steady growth since the beginning of the 80s. Experts all over the world believe that the economy's potential for even faster growth is quite strong. A view is gaining ground that India will become one of the dominant economies of the world by the mid-twenty-first century. With a faster rise in per capita incomes, the curse of widespread poverty is also expected to disappear.

There is no doubt that India's economy is currently on a new growth path. Part of the reason for the resurgence of confidence in India's future is the process of economic reforms initiated in 1991. However, there is another important reason why there has been such a dramatic shift in India's economic outlook. The basic reason, which is sometimes overlooked, is that the sources of comparative advantage of nations are vastly different today than they were even twenty years ago. There are very few developing countries that are as well placed as India to take advantage of the phenomenal changes that have occurred in production technologies, international trade, capital movement and the deployment of skilled manpower. As a result, India today has the knowledge and skills to produce and process a wide variety of products and services at competitive costs.

Periodic elections to seek the people's mandate for the government to continue in office (or otherwise), are truly a matter of triumph for India's democratic traditions. In the latest national elections, held in May 2014, as many as 834 million people were entitled to vote; more than 550 million persons exercised their franchise. This was the largest democratic election ever held in the history of the world. What is also remarkable about Indian elections is that a preponderant proportion of the voters is from poor rural areas. In urban areas also, there is evidence that the poor tend to vote much more than the middle and upper classes. For all Indians, and for others interested in democratic elections, it is exhilarating to see all candidates, including powerful ministers and party leaders, campaigning from time to time for the people's vote with the utmost humility and respect.

One of the most remarkable political developments since Independence was the passage of the 73rd Amendment to the Indian Constitution in 1993. As is well known, this Amendment created a new tier of local government which, within a relatively short time—by the year 2003—led to the constitution of as many as 2,35,000 new village governing institutions, i.e. gram panchayats, staffed by over 2 million elected representatives. This is probably the largest number of persons elected to serve as people's representatives in any democracy in the world. Further, as a remarkable experiment in affirmative action, the 73rd Amendment mandated that close to half of the elected positions be reserved for traditionally disadvantaged population groups (lower caste groups and women).

As we look ahead, over the long term, India now has tremendous opportunities to completely alleviate poverty and to become one of the strongest democratic global powers. To achieve this goal and meet the challenges that lie ahead, we also need to initiate some political reforms which may take some time to implement after the discussion and adoption of necessary legislative measures by the Parliament and state assemblies.

Today, we are fortunate to have a government in power, which, after twenty-five years of relatively short-term governments or non-performing coalitions of multiple parties since 1989, has a majority of its own. We now have the ability to initiate reforms in the political and administrative system which can deliver public services to the people with least diversion, delay or multi-tier corruption in the allocation of public resources.

In the past four years, the present government has initiated several key reforms, some of which have been introduced through new laws. These also had the support of parties in opposition in the Parliament. New laws included those relating to the auctions of coal and mineral mines, the Aadhaar Act, IBC and GST. The government has also liberalized FDI policies and raised the FDI cap on insurance to 49 per cent. Recently, in order to reduce the large percentage of NPAs in the banking sector, an ordinance was also issued to help banks resolve some of the bad loans, especially in cases where coordination among multiple lenders was required to curb credits to defaulting large corporate borrowers. In addition to the positive changes in law, some measures have also been taken to expand the policies for rural development and housing for the poor, and accelerate the direct delivery of various services, including subsidies through the use of technology, such as DBT. To simplify the administrative process for the delivery of public services, the number of central social sector schemes has also been pruned from 1,500 to 300, and centrally sponsored schemes have been reduced from sixty-six to twenty-eight.

Making the Right Choices

In considering future policy options, it is necessary to distinguish between 'ends' and 'means'. Thus, political freedom, alleviation of poverty, universal literacy, equal economic opportunities and so on, are objectives or 'ends'. While these objectives are non-negotiable, the specific policies or 'means' that are adopted to achieve them, are matters of choice. For example, in a fast-growing economy like India, there can be no disagreement about the need to generate more jobs or provide adequate job security for workers. However, whether the best instrument for achieving this objective is through the expansion of the public sector, is a legitimate subject for reasoned debate. Similarly, there can be no two views on the desirability of higher growth with a better distribution of income in a developing country. But there can be a legitimate difference of views on the correct degree of the trade-off between the two objectives in the short run, or the right mix of policies to achieve the agreed objectives.

For a better future, it is important to have a consensus on primary development objectives over the next few years and then have a debate on the means of achieving them. If we don't like capital markets, competition, global integration or foreign investment, then let us review their impact on the objectives that we agree on and choose the right policy-mix. Similarly, if we prefer public enterprises, or wish to confine the delivery of services to the poor, to government servants, let us examine their impact on the agreed objectives of generating more jobs and poverty alleviation, and then justify these policies on those grounds.

In light of the past experience on the slow pace of economic reforms in India, in some quarters there is a feeling that basic economic reforms are feasible only in a crisis, through a majority party government at the Centre and states. This view is not valid for two reasons. Firstly, a slower pace of reforms, based on consensus, is vastly preferable. It is also likely to be more durable in a democracy. Secondly, a severe economic or domestic crisis is highly damaging to the economy and the people. The Latin American economies, for example, which experienced severe crises from time to time, suffered a substantial and abrupt drop in their national income and employment. The adverse effects of these developments lasted for several years. The poor were the worst affected. While crisis-driven reforms may have rescued the economy in the short run, the long-term effects on growth and welfare were largely negative (compared to the counter-factual hypothesis of slow and steady reforms without a crisis).

The cost-benefit of economic policies in developing countries is likely to depend on the domestic and external conditions facing a particular country. The right choice of policies is, therefore, ultimately a matter of judgment for those responsible for taking the necessary decisions in the country. It also needs to be recognized that the validity of the chosen policy-mix has to be judged in the light of actual results on the ground and not in terms of any predetermined optimal model of growth or capital accumulation. If the chosen policies do not yield the expected results, it is desirable to modify or reverse them as early as possible rather than persist with them.

The real world is complex and the interrelationship between countries and the global economy is also changing, particularly during periods when there are significant developments in technology (e.g. the IT revolution) or political alignments (e.g. the formation of the European Economic Community or the demise of the Soviet Union). The mix of policies that are required to adjust to the changing situation cannot fit neatly into any fixed paradigm. Today's global economic and geopolitical environment is vastly different from that of the earlier decades following India's independence. It also has to be recognized that, in all societies, different sections of people have different interests and there is nothing wrong in having such interests. In modern economies, workers have their legitimate interests in job security and higher wages, just as entrepreneurs and companies have their interests in maximizing profits and market shares. Consumers have interests in adequate supply of goods and services at low prices, just as retailers and traders have interests in a strong demand and higher margins. Similarly, farmers have interests in higher food prices and governments have interests in ensuring food security at reasonable prices.

The real issue from a policy point of view is not that there are such special interests, but how these interests are reconciled with the public interest. If the pursuit of special interests leads to the adoption of policies which minimize the public welfare or which lead to higher incomes for a particular section of the people, at the expense of the economy in general, then those policies are clearly wrong and deserve to be abandoned. The need to reconcile the pursuit of legitimate private interests with the interests of the society or the people in general is the primary rationale for setting up supervisory or regulatory bodies, such as a central bank or a stock market regulator, in most economies.

An important priority in the choice of appropriate strategies and policies in a democracy is that these decisions must be based on a reasonable consensus (not necessarily unanimity) across the political spectrum. In making the right choices, we must also make a distinction between objectives (ends) and instruments (means) that need to be pursued in order to meet the agreed objectives. The merits of specific policies must be determined and debated in terms of their impact on achieving the desired economic goals rather than preconceived ideological positions. Similarly, the appropriateness of a policy needs be judged in relation to the actual results on the ground, rather than in terms of any optimal theoretical model or standard package of reforms. If the chosen policies turn out to be wrong, they must be modified or abandoned as early as possible, even if they can be justified on the grounds of preconceived notions of what is the right thing for a developing country to do. India's policies must be tested in light of what they achieve for India. Finally, it has to be recognized that different sections of the people have legitimate economic interests which they should be free to pursue as per the law of the land. However, if there is a conflict between private/sectional interests and the wider public interest, then the latter must prevail.

As it happens, colonial and feudal traditions are still reflected in the perquisites and various other public adornments available to government ministers. It is desirable to make these offices less attractive in terms of the public display of power, ostentation and personal staff surrounding them. There is no reason why a minister in office cannot continue to function exactly as he or she was doing prior to becoming a minister (i.e. as a MP or MLA) with some additional secretarial assistance. With ministers coming into office and going out of office with greater frequency, it would be desirable if the gap in terms of ostentation between being 'in' or 'out' is reduced. Hopefully, such a levelling of status may reduce the unseemly scramble for ministerial berths by legislators.

The concern about the need to improve government finances has figured in Budget discussions in the Parliament and outside for more than four decades (i.e. after the first oil crisis in 1973, when stringent expenditure control measures had to be introduced to release resources for oil imports). Numerous committees and commissions, including finance commissions, have made appropriate recommendations to improve budgetary receipts and reduce expenditure. Governments, both at the Centre and states, have also taken several steps to improve the fiscal situation. An important initiative taken by the government is the adoption of the FRBM Act. Under the Act, annual and lower ceilings have to be announced by the government in respect of both fiscal and revenue deficits, until the desired targets are reached. From the long-run point of view, this is a commendable and welcome step.

It is, however, likely that the positive effects of the fiscal responsibility legislation, in improving the government's ability to undertake higher expenditure in vital public areas, will take some time. This is because the government's access to market borrowings and its revenue expenditure needs to be substantially reduced in order to meet the lower annual targets of fiscal and revenue deficits. Part of the gap may be covered by revenue buoyancy due to tax reforms. However, the government's overall expenditure would have to grow at a much lower rate than before.

There is no easy way out of this dilemma in view of the excesses of the past. The only possible way out for the government, in the next few years, is to sell its idle or loss-making assets and reduce its unproductive organizational expenditure. In view of the political compulsions, the choice is difficult. But this is the only choice. The government would do well to evolve a consensus on this score as early as possible, by fully protecting the interests of government employees and other parastatal organizations. The government should give an assurance that, while all its employees would have the option to avail themselves of a generous Voluntary Retirement Scheme, they could also continue as employees of the government if they wish, and draw their full salaries and other benefits. Those who opt for the second alternative would be treated as employees 'on leave awaiting fresh postings'. Even if full salaries are paid, the cash position of the government would still improve substantially because of receipts from asset sales and elimination of non-salary office expenditure. In several government enterprises, annual cash losses are, in any case, substantially higher than salaries.

Substantial savings, and the reduction of corruption and the harassment faced by the public are possible by reducing the large number of government organizations and 'attached' offices which no longer serve any useful purpose. It is unnecessary to individually list such organizations, but even a cursory look at the list of central or state government offices in the local telephone directory would provide sufficient evidence of the non-functionality of the vast superstructure of a large number of attached offices of government. These were set up years ago for promotional, information or productivity improvement work, but have now become moribund. Large savings are possible by reducing the size of this superstructure without adversely affecting the interests of the staff or those of the public.

There is now agreement among all sections of the country, including political leaders, judges and civil servants, on the urgent need for legal and administrative reforms. The consensus on this objective has been evident, in varying degrees, over the past few decades. In response to the perceived need, several commissions have been set up; recommendations have been put forward by periodical high-level conferences of presiding officers of state legislatures and the Houses of Parliament former Chief Justices of the Supreme Court and high courts have made observations; civil service organizations have passed resolutions; and experts and journalists have written extensively in the media. Nevertheless, by all accounts, the legal delays in delivering justice, and administrative problems in delivering citizens' entitlements, have continued to mount.

In future—say, by 2025—if there is sufficient will and cooperation among different branches, i.e. the legislature, judiciary and executive, it should be politically less difficult to devise solutions to the problem of legal delays. This is because various interests, which are likely to be adversely affected by the reduction of legal delays, are widely dispersed and it may not be feasible to evolve a united opposition towards measures for reform. A number of commissions, including law commissions, have already made a large number of recommendations for expediting the disposal of cases, and some of these have been implemented. However, the progress in reducing delays, particularly at the levels of the high courts and lower rungs of the judiciary, has been very slow.

An important part of the problem is the plethora of legislative provisions on all respects of national life, some of which are more than one hundred years old and internally contradictory. The vast legislative framework, as it has evolved over the past century or more, provides a fertile ground for continuous litigation by unscrupulous persons and organizations. This is an area where a special and time-bound standing committee of the Parliament, set up for the purpose of reducing and simplifying legislative provisions in areas where the pressure of litigation is high, can make an important contribution.

A step by which the judiciary itself can take the initiative, is reducing the number of non-working days and the length of court vacations. The decision to increase the number of working days may be combined with the enforcement of strict limitations on the facility for multiple appeals, adjournments and frequent hearings at different levels of the judiciary. It is also desirable to delink judicial salaries from those of the civil services and relate them to conditions prevailing in the legal profession. A workable and non-discretionary formula can be evolved by relating judges' salaries at various levels to those of the top ten or twenty lawyers practising in different courts.

Legal reforms to reduce delays should not present an insurmountable difficulty if there is an agreement among the different branches not only on the need for expediting judicial processes, but also on the urgency of doing so. Administrative reforms, on the other hand, are likely to face greater political opposition as special interests in this area are united, unionized and affiliated to various political parties. However, if the legitimate interests of employees in the government and parastatal organizations are protected, and the economic costs of continuing with the present system are recognized, it may be possible to evolve a political consensus to reduce administrative bottlenecks, if not eliminate them.

It may be noted that there were significant successes in some areas where an effort was made in the past to replace old and cumbersome administrative procedures. One such example is the procedural reforms introduced in the mid-1980s in respect of the grant of pensions for government employees. Earlier, the system was so paper-ridden that it used to take a year or more before a retiree could claim his or her pension. After the revamp of the system, such delays were completely eliminated. Another example is that of reforms introduced in the approval system, applicable to foreign exchange releases over the past two decades. Earlier, every such release had to be referred to the central bank of the country, through an authorized dealer, which in turn referred it to the government, when necessary. In addition to substantial delays and uncertainties, the earlier procedures had given rise to a corruption industry centred on foreign exchange markets (including the emergence of a flourishing illegal 'hawala'[14]

---

[14]Hawala market is defined as money transfers by groups of brokers and others,

market). The old system has now been replaced by a rule-based system largely dependent on self-certification. The new system has resulted in substantial economic gains in the management of the country's foreign exchange resources.

These are only a couple of examples where the bypassing of the old system yielded noticeable benefits. There are similar examples of administrative reforms in other areas, as mentioned in earlier chapters. Such successful examples deserve to be replicated over the entire administrative spectrum. Along with decentralization and citizens' right to information, the adoption of the best practices for the delivery of services should result in substantial cost efficiencies and reduction in corruption. These, in turn, would significantly raise the country's rate of growth.

In recent years, a great deal has been written about globalization, both on its merits and its discontents. The issue has also figured prominently in the debate on economic policy in India in the context of the 'opening up' of the economy to international trade and much larger inflows of foreign investments in the post-1990 period. Internationally, as well as in India, the term 'globalization' has been used in a variety of ways, and views about its merits or demerits have depended crucially on how it has been defined. In one sense, it merely represents a fact of life, i.e. geographical distances between nations are no longer as important as they used to be, in defining national identities or national advantages. The world has shrunk and no nation can remain in economic isolation from the rest of the world without hurting itself. A corollary of this view is that the integration of world markets is beneficial for all participating economies, just

---

among themselves, without making actual remittances of foreign exchange through banking channels.

as a more competitive and larger domestic market is beneficial for a national economy.

In another, quite different sense, the word 'globalization' is used to represent a shift in domestic policies which, in some ill-defined way, makes the national interest subsidiary to interests of other countries or multinational corporations. It is feared that opening the country to international trade or international investment will integrate an economically weak country to a group of more economically powerful countries. The powerful can then take advantage of the weak, to siphon off profits and incomes from the latter. In a more political sense, greater participation in world markets is believed to represent economic dependence on dominant world powers, which in turn, is expected to lead to political dependence. It has then been argued that an inevitable consequence of economic integration would be a clear loss of autonomy. This argument is part of a broader critique of market-based development, which is supposed to work only in favour of the middle- and upper-income groups. Such development, it has been suggested, leads to the marginalization of the weak and the poor.

Against the above background, in considering the costs and benefits of globalization in the Indian context, a few points should be kept firmly in view. First, the cost-benefits are entirely a function of what kind of globalization policy a country has adopted. In considering the merits of closer integration of a developing economy with the global economy, it is desirable to avoid the use of the word 'globalization' altogether. It is much more rational to specify the precise content of the policies that are under consideration, for example, import liberalization, financial liberalization, capital account convertibility, removal of restrictions on FDI, and so on. In the absence of such specification, it is possible to put forward widely different positions on the subject of globalization in general terms, with seemingly equal justification.

Second, in order to bring about closer integration of national economies, specific policies in respect of trade, investment, capital markets, and so on, have to be carefully 'managed' in its own interest, by the country concerned. As it happens, all national economies or regional economic formations pursue different policies in order to maximize their own benefits. Thus, for example, industrial countries are in favour of freer trade in industrial goods, but not necessarily in agriculture or services. Similarly, economies with a dominant and large financial or banking sector may favour external financial liberalization, but not necessarily in their domestic capital markets. India should also adopt policies which maximize the national advantage (including that of countries which are similarly situated) in an international framework.

Third, in considering the possible adverse effects of greater openness in trade or investment, it is important to bear in mind that, despite some positive movement in these areas over the past two decades, India is nowhere near integrating with the world, or being 'absorbed' by foreign powers. By any measure, China—a communist country with an independent foreign policy—is more integrated with the world economy than India is, or is likely to be in the foreseeable future. The annual FDI in China, by overseas companies, is substantially higher than their investment in India. China, no doubt, has its economic and political problems, but a loss of autonomy or erosion in the authority of the State, due to its participation in foreign trade and foreign investment, is certainly not among them. Since all major developing countries are aggressively pursuing policies to increase their share of world trade and FDI, India's relative share is unlikely to reach anywhere near China's present share for quite some time.

India's policies in respect of the global economy should be framed in the light of the above considerations. While there is certainly a good reason to be cautious about 'across the board' financial and capital account liberalization, the fears of economic dependence due to trade and foreign investment are simply irrelevant in today's conditions. In respect of capital account also, a substantial movement forward is now feasible in view of India's strong BoP position and a competitive domestic environment. The possibility of external pressures, resulting in damage to national prosperity, is likely to become more real in stagnant and closed economies than in economies that are expanding by exploiting new opportunities in trade and technology. This is vividly illustrated by India's own varied experience in the past and the present, and is likely to hold true in the future also.

As we look to India's challenges and opportunities over the long run, it is possible to be daunted by the complex set of problems that a fast-growing developing country faces in the global economy. On the other hand, as we reflect on what we have been able to achieve through a participatory, open and democratic society, there are sufficient reasons to be cheerful and confident. In recent years, the global environment has also changed in India's favour. There are very few developing countries that are as well placed as India to take advantage of the phenomenal changes that have occurred in technology, international trade, capital movement and sources of comparative advantage of nations. Like never before, India's destiny is now truly in the hands of its people. With the determination to realize the country's vast potential, India's economy can become one of the strongest in the world in the not-too-distant future. Widespread poverty, illiteracy and disease would then largely disappear and democracy would have given the people their just rewards.

Acknowledgements

This book could not have been written without the guidance and advice of Yamini Chowdhury, Senior Commissioning Editor with Rupa Publications India. She was kind enough to collaborate with me to decide on the contents of the book and give her advice on the possible reforms needed for India to make, what she referred to as 'a great leap in the next century'.

I am also grateful to Satish Choudhary for his painstaking work in putting together the manuscript of this book for publication, and to K.D. Sharma for his help.

Index

Aadhaar Act, 139
Action taken reports, 36
Administrative procedures, simplification of, 21
Administrative reforms, xvii, 112–26, 145, 147–48
Administrative system, 117–18
Agrobased activities, 131
Anti-corruption strategies, 67–74
   demand-side measures, 73–74
   essential component, 68–69
   institutional reform, 67
   need for institutional reform, 68–69
   penalties, 67–68
   supply-side measures, 69–72
Anti-defection law, xiv, 45–46
Asian financial crisis (1997), xvi, 19
Association for Democratic Reforms (ADR), 51
Autonomy, 25, 65, 123, 149–150

Balance of payments (BoP), 19, 96–97, 110, 114, 128, 151
Banking industry
   competitive conditions, 98
   loans, interest rate subsidies on, 97
   long-term vision for, 106
   rate, reactivated, 98
Basel Committee, 99
Basic structure doctrine, 40–41
Black money, 58
Bribery or the funding of parties, 43
Budget and finance bill, 18
Budgetary receipts, 143
Bureaucracy
   dominant role of, 117
   proliferation of, 118

Capital account convertibility, 93, 108, 149
Capital adequacy ratio, 99–100

Capital movement, ix, 93, 134, 137, 151
Cash reserve ratio (CRR), 96–97
Central Bureau of Investigation, 58
Chit funds, 104
Civil administration, politicization of, 44
Civil services
    depoliticization of, 24–26
    empowerment of, 25, 123
Civil society institutions, 22, 72, 120
Coalition government, 2, 4–5, 14, 16, 45, 52, 56
Coalition of parties, x, 17, 116
Coalition politics, 4, 31, 38, 42
Coalitions and the parliament, 42–46
    post-election allies, 42
    splits among parties, 43
Competitive politics, 48
Comprehensive Rural Health Project, 82
Compulsions and Pressures of Power, 54–56
Constitution of India, 3
    73rd and 74th amendments, 65, 138
    concurrent list, 3
    framers foresight, 3
    state list, 3
Consumer Price Index (CPI), 83
Controls on capital issues, abolition of, 97

Corruption
    bureaucratic, 60, 124
    cause of fiscal drain, 66
    components, 73
    economic effects, 61–67
    higher inflation, 66
    hurdle in growth, 61
    index, 62, 67
    multi-tier, 2, 135, 139
    politicization of, 61
    'retail' component, 73
    supply and demand of, 60–61
    vertical integration of, 60
    zero tolerance of, 57–59
Corruption multiplier, 59
    damaging effects of the, xv
    worst effect of, 59
Corruption Perceptions Index, 57, 67
Council of States, 6–9
Criminal misconduct, definition of, 58
Criminals in politics, xiv, 47–56
    dominance of, 50–52
Crisis-driven reforms, 141
Cross-voting, 43, 54

Decentralization, xvi, 88
Defections, 15–16
Democratic norms and conventions, violation of, 31
Depreciating currency, headline effect of a, 109
Direct Benefit Transfers (DBT), 58, 77, 139

Index

Domestic inflation, 109
Domestic policies, 149
Duality of India, 32

East Asian crisis (1997), 91–95
   exchange rate policies, 92
   handling capital flows, 93
   proximate cause, 93
   rescue effort, 92
E-commerce, 107
Economic policies, cost-benefit of, 141
Economic power concentration in a business houses, 113
Economic reforms, 73, 75–76, 118–19, 137, 140
   slow pace of, 140
Economy, growth performance, 20, 134–35
Education for all, 85–86
E-governance, 58
Election Commission of India (EC), 11
Electoral agenda, x
Electoral funding
   problems of, 12
   transparency in, 13
Electoral process, reform of, 8
Electronic real-time gross settlement system, 108
Emergency in 1975–77, 15, 40
Employment opportunities, 131, 135
European Economic Community, 141

Exchange rate, 92, 94, 96, 98, 108–11

Feudal traditions, 143
Finance Commission, 5, 124
Financial consolidation, 100
Financial intermediaries, emergence of, 103
Financial liberalization, 149–50
Financial markets, globalization of, 101
Financial powers, 5, 49, 89
   centralization of, 88
   decentralization of, xvi
Financial resources, 5
Financial sector reforms, domestic, 97
Fiscal deficit, 26–28, 66, 94, 115
Fiscal empowerment, 26–28
   fiscal deficits, 26–27
Fiscal Responsibility and Budget Management (FRBM) Act, 26, 144
Fiscal stringency, 28, 80
Food security, 82–85
Foreign direct investment (FDI), 98, 131, 139, 149–51
   cap on insurance, 139
   liberalized policies, 139
Foreign exchange resources, 148
Foreign investment, 113, 128, 130–31, 140, 148, 150–51
Foreign trade, 110, 128, 150
Foreign travels of government officials, 58

Free media, 22, 72, 120
Fundamental rights, 40
Future priorities, 118–26
   accountability of civil servants, 123
   administrative priority, 120
   macroeconomic priorities, 120
   rule-based system of administration, 123
   simplify administrative procedures, 121–22
   transparency in the decision-making process, 120

Gandhi, Rajiv, 64
Global Corruption Barometer, xv, 57
Goods and Services Tax (GST), 4
Governance, crisis of, 19
Gross Domestic Product (GDP) ratio, xvii
GST, 77, 125, 139

Hawala market, 147
Health services
   delivery of, xvi, 87–88
   equitable access, 86–89
High Court Arrears Committees, 68
Horizontal spread of corruption, 60
Human Development Index (HDI), xv, 77–78

Ideological or electoral agenda, x

Illicit wealth, accumulation of, xi, 9
Indian Penal Code, 51
Inflation, xv, 21, 66, 83, 108–9, 120
Insolvency and Bankruptcy Code (IBC), 102–3, 139
Institutional reforms, 76, 103
International Monetary Fund (IMF), 62, 92, 96
Interstate disputes, 4
Interventionist strategies, 129
Investments, allocation of, 2
IT revolution, 141

Judicial
   delays, xii, 28
   salaries, 146

Law Commission, 68, 146
Legal and Judicial Reforms, 28–29, 147
Legislative measures, 135, 138
Licencing and pricing controls, 73
Life expectancy, 77,
Lok Sabha elections, 2, 8, 10

Market-based reforms, 94
Market-determined exchange rate, 98
Members of Parliament Local Area Development Scheme (MPLADS), 10
Ministerial responsibility, 23–24
Mobilization and allocation of savings, agencies for, 96
Monetary policy, 108

Index

Money multiplier, 59
Multiparty coalitions, 4, 29, 45
   implications of, 45

Narasimham Committee, 97
National Advisory Council
   (NAC), 35, 37
National Commission to review the working of the Constitution (NCRWC), xiii, 31
National Democratic Alliance (NDA), 16
National Election Watch (NEW), 51
National Food for Work Programme, 64
National Healthcare Standards Organization, 88
National Housing Bank, 104
Natural justice, principle of, 70
Nehru, Jawaharlal, 136
New money, 108
New national health policy, 87
NITI Aayog, 5
Non-banking financial companies (NBFCs), 94, 104
Non-governmental organizations (NGOs), xii, xvi, 9, 22, 33, 72, 75, 82, 89
Non-performing Assets (NPAs), xvii, xvii, 100, 102–03, 139

Office of profit (OoP), 34–35, 37
Official Secrets Act (OSA), 25–26, 70–71

Oil crisis (1973), 143
Old-age pension, 79
Opinion polls, 19
Opposition, role of the, 38–39
Organizational reforms, xvi, 88

Palkhivala, Nani, 40
Parliament, Diminishing Role of, 32–37
Parliamentary democracy, 8, 14–15, 17
   fundamental principles of, 14
Per capita availability of food, 78
Per capita income, 67, 86, 112, 114, 127, 135, 137
Policies, liberalization of, 97
Policy-mix, 140–41
Political agenda, x
Political corruption, x, 9, 24, 53, 71, 124
Political instability, 10, 14, 16, 71
Political opportunism, x
Political power, organizational structure of, 48
Political pyramid, 49
Political reforms, xi, 2, 29, 135, 138
Political uncertainty, 15
Portfolio investment, 98
Poverty
   elimination, 127
   line, 127
   trap, 63
Pradhan Mantri Jan-Dhan Yojana, 77

Prevention of Corruption Act, 57
Private capital flows, explosion in, 101
Prudential regulation and supervision, 98
Public Affairs Centre, 19
Public Distribution System (PDS), ix, xvi, 83–85
  expansion of the, 79
  legitimate criticism of, 83
  urban bias of, 84
Public Sector, performance of, 115–17
Public services, decentralization of, xvi

Quality of Life, xv, 77–90
Question hours, 39

Rangarajan, C., 97
Red tape, 21, 121–22
Repos, 98
Representation of the People Act, 53–54
  amendments, 6–7
Right to Information (RTI), 22, 26, 58–59, 120
Role of Small Parties, 13–16
Rules of Procedure and Conduct of Business, 33

Self Employed Women's Association, 82
Sen, Amartya, 83
Separation of powers, 24–25, 123

Services revolution, 132–35
  expansion of jobs and income, 133
  growth opportunities, 133–34
  role of services, 132–33
Skill-based education, 132
Skill-based services, 132, 134
Skills-related value addition, 132
Social assistance schemes, 79
Social expenditures, 80
Standard of Living, 77
Starred questions, 39
Start-up firms, 63
State funding of elections, 9–13, 52–54
  budget expenditure, size of, 10
  equitable distribution of electoral funds, 10–12
  legitimate electoral expenses, 10
State legislatures, role of, 41
Statutory liquidity ratio (SLR), 96–97
Subsidies, xi, 22, 27, 77, 81, 125, 139
Substantial savings, 145
Sustainable Development Goals, 78

Tax resources, division of, 5
Technological change, 130
Transparency International, 57

Union Public Service Commission (UPSC), 6, 121
United Nations Convention

Index

against Corruption, 58
United Nations Development Programme, xv, 77
United Progressive Alliance (UPA), 16
Unity in Diversity, goals of, 31
Universal literacy, goal of, 86

Voice vote, xiii, 17, 35
Voluntary Retirement Scheme, 144
Vote-on-account, 18

Welfare schemes, 49
Wholesale corruption, 73
World Bank, ix, 62, 92, 118, 127